CONTENTS

CONTENTS

THE DICTIONARY OF
OUTRAGEOUS
QUOTATIONS

COMPILED AND INTRODUCED BY C.R.S. MARSDEN

Salem House Publishers

TOPSFIELD, MASSACHUSETTS

This edition first published in Great Britain by
Xanadu Publications Ltd 1988
First published in the United States by Salem House
Publishers, 1988, 462 Boston Street, Topsfield, MA 01983.

Library of Congress Cataloging-in-Publication Data

The Dictionary of outrageous quotations.
   1. Quotations, English. I. Marsden, C.R.S.,
1944–
PN6081.D528   1988   808.8′2   87-35586
ISBN 0-88162-367-9

Printed and bound in Great Britain

CONTENTS

INTRODUCTION

Outrage is not a unitary thing. People can be outraged in many different ways. A paradox is a logical outrage; blasphemy is a theological outrage; insults are outrages to personal or collective sacred identities; obscenities outrage verbal etiquette or moral imperatives; and lies outrage our common sense of truthfulness.

Having only one rule of selection would produce the tedium of lettuce with everything, so I have drawn on all these sources of outrage – and from a wide range of times and cultures, for outrage is not only relative to the persons involved but it also waxes and wanes with the spirit and values of the historical moment. When George Bernard Shaw made his remark about Queen Victoria and the parlourmaid he no doubt intended to outrage royalists; nowadays we might be more appalled by his patronizing attitude to parlourmaids. Context, too – or the lack of it – may contribute to the outrageousness of some of these quotations, and while I have supplied supporting information where it is needed, too much explanation would spoil the joke. If this is unfair in some cases, so be it.

Overall, though, I have assumed that the reader will be aware of the relationship between the quote and the speaker, and of the presuppositions which frame it – for it is often this incompatibility, self-contradiction or clash of assumptions that causes the outrage. For example, if a politician says 'We shall seek out corruption and dishonesty wherever it may hide, and fearlessly expose it to the public judgement,' any outrageousness may well depend on knowing that the same politician was expelled from college for cheating, received massive personal payments while in public office in return for legislative and contract-fixing favours, and ran a dirty tricks squad which framed opponents for murder, child-abuse and treason.

Most collections of quotations consist overwhelmingly of clever statements of received, invented or discovered wisdom, or just wisecracks. I hope that this collection is somewhat more pointed, and the only apology I make is that, within the constraints of time and a limited number of pages, it can only be a sampler; I'm particularly aware that I might have done less than justice to contemporary foot-in-mouth artists and obscene designers whose work deserves to be celebrated and appreciated in the context of other filth, blasphemy, bigotry and offensiveness. To this end I invite readers to send their own specimens c/o the publisher, and we'll see where *that* takes us.

– C. R. S. MARSDEN

ADVERTISING

'A boy's gotta hustle his book.' – TRUMAN CAPOTE

'Advertising is the rattling of a stick inside a swill bucket.'
– GEORGE ORWELL

'When I had looked at the lights of Broadway by night, I said to my American friends: "What a glorious garden of wonders this would be, to any one who was lucky enough to be unable to read." ' – G. K. CHESTERTON

'Advertising may be described as the science of arresting the human intelligence long enough to get money from it.'
– STEPHEN LEACOCK

'Unmentionables – those articles of ladies' apparel that are never discussed in public, except in full-page, illustrated ads.' – *Changing Times*

'Advertising, in its spirit and purpose, is germinal fascism. Hitler was the first European politician who saw the significance of the techniques of commercial advertising for politics.' – J. B. MATTHEWS and R. E. SHALLCROSS

'Freedom! To spit in the eye and in the soul of the passerby and the passenger with advertising.'
– ALEXANDER SOLZHENITSYN

AMERICA

'What a pity, when Christopher Columbus discovered America, that he ever mentioned it.' – MARGOT ASQUITH

'I am willing to love all mankind, except an American.'
– DR JOHNSON

'America is a large, friendly dog in a very small room. Every time it wags its tail it knocks over a chair.'
– ARNOLD TOYNBEE

'America is part – and a great part – of the Greater Britain which seems so plainly destined to dominate this planet!'
– *New York Times* (1897)

'We must keep America whole and safe and unspoiled.'
–AL CAPONE

'The United States will collapse by 1980.'
– TIMOTHY LEARY (1965)

'Soak it in heroin and I'll suck it.'
– WILLIAM BURROUGHS, on the American flag

'The people of America are just not born with culture.'
– PHIL SPECTOR

'I have entertained on sundry occasions that sort of feeling for an American woman which the close vicinity of an unclean animal produces.'   – ANTHONY TROLLOPE (1861)

'I epitomize America.'   – JOHN DENVER

'The toilet paper there is so thin you have to use three sheets and the beer tastes like weasel piss.'   – JOE JACKSON

'Fuck your Parliament and your constitution. America is an elephant. Cyprus is a flea. Greece is a flea. If these two fellows continue itching the elephant, they may just get whacked by the elephant's trunk, whacked good . . . If your Prime Minister gives me talk about democracy, Parliament and constitution, he, his parliament and his constitution may not last very long.'

– PRESIDENT LYNDON JOHNSON,
to the Greek Ambasssador to the USA in
1965, two years before the Colonel's
military coup in Greece.

'Losing is the great American sin.'   – JOHN TUNIS

'America is a land where a citizen will cross the ocean to fight for democracy – and won't even cross the street to vote in a national election.'   – BILL VAUGHAN

'You hear about constitutional rights, free speech, and the free press. Every time I hear these words I say to myself, "That man is a Red, that man is a Communist!" You never hear a real American talk like that.'

– MAYOR FRANK HAGUE

'I don't feel we did wrong in taking this great country away from them. There were great numbers of people who needed new land, and the Indians were selfishly trying to keep it for themselves.' – JOHN WAYNE

'I don't see much future for the Americans . . . Everything about the behaviour of American society reveals that it's half judaized, and the other half negrified. How can one expect a state like that to hold together?' – ADOLPH HITLER

'I confess that I cannot understand how we can plot, lie, cheat and commit murder abroad and remain human, honorable, trustworthy and trusted at home.' – ARCHIBALD COX

'This country will not be a good place for any of us to live in unless we make it a good place for all of us to live in.' – THEODORE ROOSEVELT

'This land of ours cannot be a good place for any of us to live in unless it is a good place for all of us to live in.' – RICHARD NIXON

'America is a mistake, a giant mistake!'   – SIGMUND FREUD

'I don't know much about Americanism, but it's a damn good word with which to carry an election.' – WARREN G. HARDING

'No one ever went broke underestimating the taste of the American public.'   – H. L. MENCKEN

'It could probably be shown by facts and figures that there is no distinctively American criminal class except Congress.'   – MARK TWAIN

HOLLYWOOD

'Hollywood: They know only one word of more than one syllable there, and that is "fillum".'   – LOUIS SHERWIN'

'Hollywood: A place where the inmates are in charge of the asylum.'   – ascribed to LAURENCE STALLINGS

'Behind the phoney tinsel of Hollywood lies the real tinsel.'   – OSCAR LEVANT

'I'm a Hollywood writer; so I put on a sports jacket and take off my brain.'   – BEN HECHT

Los Angeles

'Los Angeles is like one of those machines that treat flour. When the wheat comes in, it's full of interesting ingredients – but it goes through this machine and what you get out at the end is perfect white crap.'   – BRIAN ENO

'Los Angeles should be wiped off the face of the earth.'   – DAVID BOWIE

'LA is a meat factory that grinds people into neat little packages. I didn't want to be a neat little package.'

– KEITH MOON, explaining why he left

'LA you pass though and get a hamburger.'

– JOHN LENNON

New York

'I don't like the life in New York. There is no greenery. It would make a stone sick.'   – NIKITA KRUSCHEV

'This muck heaves and palpitates. It is multidirectional and has a mayor.'   – DONALD BARTHELME

ANIMALS, BIRDS, BEES etc.

'A Portsmouth man believes he has found the way to talk to hedgehogs – although he does not know the meaning of what he says to them.'   – *Evening News*

'There is one thing I like doing and that's putting a mouse to your ear and having it breathe very rapidly into your ear – it's great, it's very exciting.'   – JILTED JOHN

'Better the chill blast of winter than the hot breath of a pursuing elephant.'   – CHINESE PROVERB

'We hope that, when the insects take over the world, they will remember with gratitude how we took them along on all our picnics.'   – BILL VAUGHAN

'We Germans, who are the only people in the world who have a decent attitude toward animals, will also assume a decent attitude toward these human animals.'
– HEINRICH HIMMLER

'Bees are not as busy as we think they are. They just can't buzz any slower.'　　　– FRANK 'KIN' HUBBARD

'The armchair ornithophil stirs enviously as he reads of watching a skua standing on a kittiwake's back, murdering it slowly by eating its neck.'　　　– From review in *The Observer*

'A hen is only an egg's way of making another egg.'
– SAMUEL BUTLER

ART

'The history of art, like all history, is to a large extent an agreed fable.'　　　– SIR KENNETH CLARKE

'The new job of art is to sit on the wall and get more expensive.'　　　– ROBERT HUGHES

'Art, if there is such a thing, is in the bathrooms – everybody knows that.'　　　– BOB DYLAN

'Art? Art? All the art in the world isn't worth a good meat and potato pie.'　　　– L. S. LOWRY

'What is art? Prostitution.'   – CHARLES BAUDELAIRE

'It does not matter how badly you paint so long as you
don't paint badly like other people.'   – GEORGE MOORE

'A doctor can bury his mistakes but an architect can only
advise his client to plant vines.'   – FRANK LLOYD WRIGHT

'He bores me. He ought to have stuck to his flying
machines.'   – AUGUSTE RENOIR, on Leonardo da Vinci

'All day long I add up columns of figures and make everything balance. I come home. I sit down. I look at a
Kadinsky and it's wonderful! It doesn't mean a damn
thing!'   – SOLOMAN GUGGENHEIM

'Less is more.'   – MIES VAN DER ROHE

'Artists can color the sky red because they know it's blue.
Those of us who aren't artists must color things the way
they really are or people might think we're stupid.'
                                    – JULES FEIFER

'Anyone who sees and paints a sky green and pastures blue
ought to be sterilized.'   – ADOLF HITLER

BED

'I don't like lying awake, it does no good. I make it a point
never to lie awake.'   – DUKE OF WELLINGTON

'A lady was awoke in the night with the disagreeable sense of not being alone in the room, and soon felt a thud upon her bed. There was no doubt that someone was moving to and fro in the room, and that hands were constantly moving over her bed. She was so dreadfully frightened that at last she fainted. When she came to herself, it was broad daylight, and she found that the butler had walked in his sleep and had laid the table for fourteen upon her bed.'

– AUGUSTUS J. C. HARE (1880)

'Sleeping alone, except under doctor's orders, does much harm. Children will tell you how lonely it is sleeping alone. If possible you should always sleep with someone you love. You both recharge your mutual batteries free of charge.'   – MARLENE DIETRICH

'I have never been able to sleep with anyone. I require a full-size bed so that I can lie in the middle of it and extend my arms spreadeagle on both sides without being obstructed.'   – MAE WEST

'I think you should always laugh in bed – people always laugh at me when I'm in bed.'   – BOY GEORGE

BUSINESS

'Nobody talks more of free enterprise and competition and of the best man winning than the man who inherited his father's store or farm.'   – C. WRIGHT MILLS

'All I was ever concerned about was the workforce in Northern Ireland.'
                                            – JOHN DE LOREAN

'Private enterprise . . . makes OK private action which would be considered dishonest in public action.'
                                            – JOHN F. KENNEDY

'We stand for the maintenance of private property . . . We shall protect free enterprise as the most expedient, or rather the sole possible economic order.'   – ADOLF HITLER

'You never expected justice from a company, did you? They have neither a soul to lose, nor a body to kick.'
                                            – SYDNEY SMITH

'Hell hath no fury like a bureaucrat scorned.'
                                            – MILTON FRIEDMAN

'We're against bureaucracy, hypocrisy and anything ending in Y.'   – JOHNNY ROTTEN

CANADA

'Canada is useful only to provide me with furs.'
                                            – MADAME DE POMPADOUR

'I don't even know what street Canada is on.'
                                            – AL CAPONE

'Canada is a country so square that even the female imper-sonators are women.'

– RICHARD BENNER, in the movie *Outrageous*

'You have to know a man awfully well in Canada to know his surname.'   – JOHN BUCHAN

CENSORSHIP

'I am going to introduce a resolution to have the Postmas-ter General stop reading dirty books and deliver the mail.'

– GAIL McGEE

'A sodomite got very excited looking at a zoology text. Does this make it pornography?'   – STANISLAW J. LEC

CHILDREN

'The servant has come for the little Browns this morning – they have been a toothache to me which I shall enjoy the riddance of – Their little voices are like wasps' stings.'

– JOHN KEATS

'Parents are the very last people who ought to be allowed to have children.'   – H. E. BELL

'I was much distressed by next door people who had twin

babies and played the violin: but one of the twins died, and
the other has eaten the fiddle – so all is peace.'

– EDWARD LEAR

'I was this forenoon paying a visit to John Dalrymple. He
told me that Ferguson (Civil Society) used to maintain,
that till a child was four years old it was no better than a
cabbage.'   – JAMES BOSWELL

'I only hope that it will be of the right sex, i.e. the feminine,
as I hardly need say. I like some particular boys; but the
genus boy seems to me one of nature's mistakes. Girls
improve as they grow up; but the boy generally deterior-
ates, and, in our infernal system, has to be sent away to
school and made into more or less of a brute.'

– LESLIE STEPHEN

'I strongly support the feeding of children.'

– GERALD FORD, on the School Lunch Bill

'I have been assured by a very knowing American of my
acquaintance in London that a healthy young child, well
nursed, is at a year old a most delicious, nourishing and
wholesome food, whether stewed, roasted, baked or
boiled: and I make no doubt that it will equally serve in a
fricassee or a ragout.'   – JONATHAN SWIFT

'I love children – especially when they cry, for then someone takes them away.'   – NANCY MITFORD

'If you strike a child, take care that you strike it in anger, even at the risk of maiming it for life. A blow in cold blood neither can nor should be forgiven.'

– GEORGE BERNARD SHAW

'My mother loved children – she would have given anything if I had been one.'   – GROUCHO MARX

'The thing that impresses me most about America is the way parents obey their children.'   – DUKE OF WINDSOR

'Insanity is hereditary; you can get it from your children.'

– SAM LEVENSON

CIVILIZATION

'The principal task of civilization, its actual *raison d'être*, is to defend us against nature.'   – SIGMUND FREUD

'Civilization is the distance man has placed between himself and his excreta.'   – BRIAN ALDISS

'Sex appeal is the keynote of our civilization.'

– HENRI BERGSON, French philosopher

'The crossword puzzle threatens Western civilization. If it became widespread, it would make devastating inroads on the working hours of every rank of society.'   – *Times* (1925)

'The inventor tries to meet the demand of a crazy civilization.' – THOMAS ALVA EDISON

'The flush toilet is the basis of Western civilization.'
– ALAN COULT

'You can't say that civilization don't advance, for in every war they kill you in a new way.' – WILL ROGERS

CLASS

'I never knew the lower classes had such white skins.'
– LORD CURZON

'My favourite programme is *Mrs Dale's Diary*. I try never to miss it because it is the only way of knowing what goes on in the middle-class family.' – QUEEN MOTHER

'I lent Dostoievsky's *Crime and Punishment* to a friend to read, and when I asked him how he liked it he commented: "None of this would have happened if they have been to an English public school." ' – *Sunday Times*

'Striking stevedores in London's Victoria Dock yesterday rejected an appeal to unload 41 tons of melons going over-ripe in a British ship. The melon, they said, is not a working man's fruit.' – *News Chronicle*

'I am of royal blood, being a direct descendant of the Kings

of Munster. Unfortunately, I married beneath my station – my husband has an ironmongery business, and we live in Wimbledon. Most of our neighbours are vulgar people, and I long for more fastidious friends and surroundings. I have a natural sense of dignity. How can I get back where I belong?'
– Letter in *Sunday Dispatch*

'No one can make you feel inferior without your consent.'
– ELEANOR ROOSEVELT

CRIME AND PUNISHMENT

'Lech Walesa is not under arrest. He is staying at a Government guest house.'
– Polish Government Spokesman

'In some departments, the phrase "to go bent on you" means "to tell the truth" and that's part of the police culture.'
– MALCOLM SPARROW, on leaving the
Kent Police to lecture at Harvard

'Ignorance is no excuse for any crime except pop music (and arguably, bottled mayonnaise).
– IRMA KURTZ

'I didn't kill for a year. Mental anguish.'
– PETER SUTCLIFFE, The Yorkshire Ripper

'I favor capital punishment. It saves lives.'
– NANCY REAGAN

'When I came back to Dublin I was courtmartialed in my

absence and sentenced to death in my absence, so I said they could shoot me in my absence.'   – BRENDAN BEHAN

'The long and distressing controversy over capital punishment is very unfair to anyone meditating murder.'
– GEOFFREY FISHER

'Posterity, I am sure, will justify me.'
– JOHN WILKES BOOTH

CRITICS

'Having the critics praise you is like having the hangman say you've got a pretty neck.'   – ELI WALLACH

'I am convinced they are descendants of Attila the Hun, Hitler, and Charles Manson.'   – FRANK SINATRA, on critics

'A critic is a man created to praise greater men than himself, but he is never able to find them.'
– RICHARD LE GALLIENNE

'Critics are like eunuchs in a harem; they know how it's done, they've seen it done every day, but they're unable to do it themselves.'   – BRENDAN BEHAN

'A drama critic is a man who leaves no turn unstoned.'
– GEORGE BERNARD SHAW

'Asking a working writer what he feels about critics is like asking a lamp-post what it feels about dogs.'
– JOHN OSBORNE

CULTURE

'I think Michael Jackson's made greater cultural break-throughs than anyone else who's around at present.'
— BRIAN ENO

'When I hear the word *culture*, I reach for my revolver.'
— HERMANN GOERING

'Launch your boat, blessed youth, and flee at full speed from every form of culture.'
— EPICURUS

DEATH

'If I could drop dead right now, I'd be the happiest man alive.'
— SAMUEL GOLDWYN

'I'm not afraid to die. I just don't want to be there when it happens.'
— WOODY ALLEN

'A single death is a tragedy, a million deaths is a statistic.'
— JOSEPH STALIN

'Every morning I read the obits in *The Times*. If I'm not there, I carry on.'
— A. E. MATHEWS

DEMOCRACY

'Democracy is the art of running the circus from the monkey cage.'
— H. L. MENCKEN

'Democracy substitutes selection by the incompetent many for appointment by the corrupt few.'
— GEORGE BERNARD SHAW

'A democracy is no more than an aristocracy of orators. The people are so readily moved by demagogues that control must be exercised by the government over speech and press.'
— THOMAS HOBBES (1588–1697)

'The cry of equality pulls everyone down.'
— IRIS MURDOCH

DIPLOMACY

'Diplomacy – the patriotic art of lying for one's country.'
— AMBROSE BIERCE

'Sincere diplomacy is no more possible than dry water or wooden iron.'
— JOSEPH STALIN

'Any alliance whose purpose is not the intention to wage war is senseless and useless.'
— ADOLF HITLER

'Iran is an island of stability in one of the most volatile parts of the world.'
— JIMMY CARTER

'The Western Zionist-imperialist news media are committing the most significant oppression and cruelty ever committed against mankind.'
— HOJATOLESLAM MOADIKHAN,
Iranian Information Minister, April 1982

'I want to see peace, prosperity and happiness in my country, and I think the way we are going about it is the best way.'
— JOE CAHILL, Provisional IRA Leader,
October 1971

'The Kurds who are being executed do not belong to the Kurdish people.'
— AYATOLLAH KHOMEINI

DRINK

'I once shook hands with Pat Boone and my whole right side sobered up.'
— DEAN MARTIN

'When you're teetotal, you've got an awful feeling that everybody's your boss.'
— WILL FYFFE

'He that drinks wine drinks blood, and he that drinks water drinks phlegm.'
— FLORIO (1591)

'I'm a Catholic and I can't commit suicide, but I plan to drink myself to death.'
— JACK KEROUAC

'In the summer I drink Guinness, which requires no refrig-
eration and no cooking – Guinness is a great day-shortener.
If you get out of bed first thing and drink a glass then the
day doesn't begin until about 12.30, when you come to
again, which is nice. I try to live in a perpetual snooze.'

– QUENTIN CRISP

'I drink to make other people interesting.'

– GEORGE JEAN NATHAN

'Two reasons for drinking: one is, when you are thirsty, to
cure it; the other, when you are not thirsty, to prevent it.'

– THOMAS LOVE PEACOCK

'A woman drove me to drink and I never even had the
courtesy to thank her.' – W. C. FIELDS

'When I sell liquor, it's called bootlegging; when my pat-
rons serve it on silver trays on Lake Shore Drive, it's called
hospitality.' – AL CAPONE

'I can't handle dope too good. Tried pot one time and it
just didn't work. I tried to make it to my car and it took me
30 minutes and it wasn't but half a block away. If I smoke a
joint it's all over bar the crying. I like good whisky and
good-looking women. I'm scared to death of being stone-
cold sober . . . I'm a religious person. I used to be a preacher.
Went to the Assembly of God Bible School in Texas. I sure
don't want to go to Hell, I pray to God I don't. I think I'll
probably go to Hell if I don't change my way of living.
Give me that whisky.' – JERRY LEE LEWIS

'You must know your limitations, I drink a bottle of Jack Daniel's a day, that's mine.' – LEMMY, of Motorhead

DRUGS

'My Lords, I regret to say that this is a drug to which all the evidence shows your Lordship's House is seriously addicted; and the drug in question is tea.'
– BARONESS WOOTTON, in a debate
in the House of Lords

'The world is having a nervous breakdown. Valium is the only glue that holds it together.' – ARTHUR JANOV

'Marijuana inflames the erotic impulses and leads to revolting sex crimes . . . One girl, known for her quietness and modesty, suddenly threw all caution to the winds. She began staying out late at nights.' – *Daily Mirror* (1964)

'Like Spearmint, [marijuana] aids concentration and helps you do almost anything a little bit better. It grows hair on the palm of your hands, introduces you to a nice type of black man, overcomes impotence, improves the appetite, banishes excess fat, constipation and headaches, relieves rheumatism, lumbago, backache, fibrositis, unpleasant body odours and work. A pot nation is a powerful nation. You think Zambia's moon project is a joke. Watch them reach Mars first.' – RICHARD NEVILLE, *Play Power*

'In almost all painful maladies I have found Indian hemp by far the most useful of drugs.'   – J. RUSSELL REYNOLDS,
physician to Queen Victoria

'LSD is an awfully overrated aspirin and very similar to old people's Disneyland.'   – CAPTAIN BEEFHEART

'In a carefully-prepared, loving LSD session a woman will inevitably have several hundred orgasms.'   – DR TIMOTHY LEARY

'I can sing much better after shooting smack in both arms than after eating too much.'   – LINDA RONSTADT

'It's easier to get people off heroin than coffee.'   – DR RICHARD T. RAPPOLT,
who treats heroin addicts

'Coke isn't habit-forming. I should know – I've been using it for years.'   – TALLULAH BANKHEAD

I've never had problems with drugs, only with policemen.'   – KEITH RICHARDS

'Do the Stones use drugs? No, never.'   – MICK JAGGER

EDUCATION

'Oh! what blockheads are those wise persons who think it necessary that a child should comprehend everything he reads.'
— ROBERT SOUTHEY

'A man who has never gone to school may steal from a freight car; if he has a university education, he may steal the whole railroad.'
— THEODORE ROOSEVELT

'When a subject becomes totally obsolete we make it a required course.'
— PETER DRUCKER

'The average PhD thesis is nothing but a transference of bones from one graveyard to another.'
— J. FRANK DOBIE

'Why should we subsidize intellectual curiosity?'
— RONALD REAGAN

'Education is a method by which one acquires a higher grade of prejudices.'
— LAURENCE J. PETER

'I prefer the company of peasants because they have not been educated sufficiently to reason incorrectly.'
— MONTAIGNE (1533–92)

'I also believe that academic freedom should protect the right of a professor or student to advocate Marxism, socialism, communism, or any other minority viewpoint – no matter how distasteful to the majority, provided . . .'
— RICHARD NIXON

'What are our schools for if not indoctrination against Communism?'
– RICHARD NIXON

'Education belongs pre-eminently to the church . . . neutral or lay schools from which religion is excluded are contrary to the fundamental principles of education.'
– POPE PIUS XI

'It has yet to be proved that intelligence has any survival value.'
– ARTHUR C. CLARKE

ENGLAND

'The national sport of England is obstacle racing. People fill their rooms with useless and cumbersome furniture, and spend the rest of their lives in trying to dodge it.'
– HERBERT BEERBOHM TREE

'I think you have a cute little country.'
– RANDY NEWMAN, to an interviewer in England

'England's terrible. It has got the worst air, the worst water the worst food, the worst anything-you-wanna-name. It is the pits. Every single person in the whole country smokes cigarettes, and they all have brown teeth and rotted out gums. Everything is black from coal. The buildings are black, the streets are black, the signs are black. After you go there for two months you're wishing for the USA. You go crazy over there. We're big stars in England.'
– FEE WAYBILL, The Tubes

'This is a very horrible country, England. We invented the mackintosh, you know. We invented the flasher, the voyeur. That's what the press is about.'

– MALCOLM McCLAREN, punk rock manager

'The British race are generally the most spiteful, contrived, deceitful bunch of hypocrites to ever hit the planet.'

– JOHNNY ROTTEN, The Sex Pistols

'Trousers – it's such a stumbling word. It epitomises the British bumbling and inability to be streamlined and coherent. In the States they have pants and jeans, but in England we still have trousers.'

– ROGER RUSKIN SPEAR, Bonzo Dog Band

'The British have an umbilical cord which has never been cut and through which tea flows constantly.' – ABC

'When God wants a hard thing done, he tells it to his Englishmen.' – *Anthology of Empire*

'Chief hangman Albert Pierrepoint met trouble only once in all the hundreds of executions he carried out, and that was with a spy. "He was not an Englishman," Pierrepoint said.' – *Daily Herald*

'We are the first race in the world, and the more of the world we inherit the better it is for the human race.'

– CECIL RHODES

'It would be a great country if only you could roof it over.'
– TOURIST overheard in London
by Richard Compton Miller

'Remember that you are an Englishman and have consequently won first prize in the lottery of life.'
– CECIL RHODES

'The English instinctively admire any man who has no talent and is modest about it.'
– JAMES AGEE

FAME

'Ah just love bein' famous and ah think anybody who says they don't is full of shit.'
– JOHNNY WINTER

'I'm – along with the Queen, you know – one of the best things England's got. Me and the Queen.'
– MICK JAGGER

'I don't care what is written about me as long as it isn't true.'
– KATHERINE HEPBURN

'Fame is being insulted by Groucho Marx.'
– DENIS O'BRIEN

'My mother speaks to me once every two years and asks me when I'm going to open a drugstore.'
– WOODY ALLEN

'I don't mind if my skull ends up on a shelf, as long as it's got my name on it.'
– DEBBIE HARRY

FAMILY

'Standing, with his back to a real fireplace, the British father presents to his wife and children a picture of dignity and importance. Standing with his back to a steaming radiator, the American father looks just ordinary.'

– Daily Mirror

'In no circumstances,' the judge continued, 'can a poker be regarded as a proper instrument of domestic chastisement.'

– News of the World

'Avoid revolution or expect to get shot. Mother and I will grieve, but we will gladly buy a dinner for the National Guardsman who shot you.'

– DR PAUL WILLIAMSON,
father of a Kent State student

'I have certainly known more men destroyed by the desire to have a wife and child and to keep them in comfort than I have seen destroyed by drink or harlots.'

– WILLIAM BUTLER YEATS

'When I was a boy of fourteen, my father was so ignorant I could hardly stand to have the old man around. But when I got to be twenty-one, I was astonished at how much he had learned in seven years.'   – MARK TWAIN

'They fuck you up, your Mum and Dad . . .'

– PHILIP LARKIN

FOOD

'Life is too short to stuff a mushroom.'

– SHIRLEY CONRAN

'A dessert without cheese is like a beautiful woman with only one eye.'   – BRILLAT SAVARIN

'Watermelon – it's a good fruit. You eat, you drink, you wash your face.'   – ENRICO CARUSO

'Judging by the vast amount of cookbooks printed and sold in the United States one would think the American woman a fanatical cook. She isn't.'   – MARLENE DIETRICH

'The vulgar boil, the learned roast, an egg.'

– ALEXANDER POPE

'Cottage cheese – there's no flavour to it. It's like kissing your sister.'   – Overheard

'I was raised almost entirely on turnips and potatoes, but I think that the turnips have more to do with the effect than the potatoes.'   – MARLENE DIETRICH

'The food was so abominable that I used to cross myself before I took a mouthful. I used to say "Ian, it tastes like armpits." '   – NÖEL COWARD, on
Ian Fleming's hospitality

'Cucumber should be well sliced, and dressed with pepper and vinegar, and then thrown out, as good for nothing.'

– DR JOHNSON

'A squid, as you know of course, has ten testicles.'

– GRAHAM KERR,
The Galloping Gourmet

'Cursed is he that uses peanuts when the recipe calls for almonds.'

– CHRISTOPHER DRIVER,
An Alternative Commination

'If Elvis Presley had eaten green vegetables he'd still be alive.'

– IAN DURY

'I'm terrified by the thought of being haunted by all the animals I've eaten in my lifetime. Can you imagine it? All those cows, sheep, and chickens clucking around in white sheets?'

– LOL CREME

'A nuclear power plant is infinitely safer than eating because 300 people choke to death on food every year.'

– DIXY LEE RAY, Governor of
the State of Washington (1977)

'We all lead more pedestrian lives than we think we do. The boiling of an egg is sometimes more important than the boiling of a love affair in the end.'

– LILLIAN HELLMAN

'There's someone at every party who eats all the celery.'

– FRANK 'KIN' HUBBARD

FRANCE

'We always have been, we are and I hope that we always shall be detested in France.' – DUKE OF WELLINGTON

'I was not sick at all in coming over from Dover to Calais, upon the sea, but yet could hardly forbear spuing at the first sight of the French women; they are most of them of such a tawny, sapy, base complexion, and have such ugly faces, which they here set out with a dresse would fright the divell.' – EDWARD BROWNE (1664)

'Frenchmen are not human beings, and must under no circumstances be dealt with as such. If a German neverthe-less lowers himself to treat a Frenchman humanly, he is only doing it in order not to come down to the level of the French. The German must therefore avoid having any voluntary dealings with a Frenchman, as otherwise he is dirtying himself and the German people indelibly.'
– PFORZHEIMER ANZEIGER (1933)

'The French are just useless. They can't organize a piss-up in a brewery.' – ELTON JOHN

FRIENDS AND ENEMIES

'We should forgive our enemies, but only after they have been hanged first.' – HEINRICH HEINE

'He's the kind of man who picks his friends – to pieces.'
– MAE WEST

'Do not use a hatchet to remove a fly from your friend's forehead.'
– Chinese proverb

'He is a fine friend. He stabs you in the front.'
– LEONARD LOUIS LEVINSON

'I never hated a man enough to give him his diamonds back.'
– ZSA ZSA GABOR

'I don't like her. But don't misunderstand me: my dislike is purely platonic.'
– HERBERT BEERBOHM TREE

'Who can refute a sneer?'
– PALEY

GOD

'Isn't God a shit!'
– RANDOLPH CHURCHILL,
after reading the Bible all
the way through for a bet

'I don't believe there is total sexual satisfaction outside Jesus Christ.'
– BILLY GRAHAM

'Christ died for our sins. Dare we make his martyrdom meaningless by not committing them?'
– JULES FEIFFER

'I've never understood how God could expect his creatures to pick the one true religion by faith – it strikes me as a sloppy way to run a universe.'   – ROBERT A. HEINLEIN,
Stranger in a Strange Land

'I think there are innumerable Gods. What we on Earth call God is a little tribal God who has made an awful mess.'
– WILLIAM S. BURROUGHS

'God's doin' the jerk, and it's the jerk's fault for lettin' him do it.'   – CAPTAIN BEEFHEART

'If God's got anything better than sex to offer, he's certainly keeping it to himself.'   – STING, The Police

'I don't know if God exists, but it would be better for His reputation is He didn't.'   – JULES RENARD

'Whenever we read the obscene stories, the voluptuous debaucheries, the cruel and tortuous executions, the unrelenting vindictiveness with which more than half the Bible is filled, it would be more consistent that we call it the word of a demon than the word of God. It is a history of wickedness that has served to corrupt and brutalize mankind.'   – THOMAS PAINE
(1737–1809)

'If only God would give me some clear sign! Like making a large deposit in my name in a Swiss bank.'
– WOODY ALLEN

'The great God Ra whose shrine once covered acres is filler
now for crossword puzzle makers.' – KEITH PRESTON

'Herein we see God's great mercy . . . for the slaughter was
in all 5,517, but ten of the enemy's side were slain to one of
ours.' – NEHEMIAH WALLINGTON

'God had a divine purpose in placing this land between two
great oceans to be found by those who had a special love of
freedom and courage.' – RONALD REAGAN

'Who says I am not under the special protection of God?'
– ADOLF HITLER

'Many a sober Christian would rather admit that a wafer is
God than that God is a cruel and capricious tyrant.'
– EDWARD GIBBON (1737–94)

'I've steered clear of God. He was an incredible sadist.'
– JOHN COLLIER

'Trinity is the word for a committee god.'
– BISHOP JAMES A. PIKE

'In war, when a commander becomes so bereft of reason
and perspective that he fails to understand the dependence
of arms on divine guidance, he no longer deserves victory.'
– GENERAL DOUGLAS McARTHUR

'This doctrine of the material efficacy of prayer reduces the

Creator to a cosmic bellhop of a not very bright or reliable
kind.'
– HERBERT J. MULLER

HAPPINESS

'Pleasure chews and grinds us.'
– MONTAIGNE

'Happiness is peace after strife, the overcoming of difficulties, the feeling of security and well-being. The only really
happy folk are married women and single men.'
– H. L. MENCKEN

'There is no logical answer to a guffaw.'
– ARNOLD BENNETT

'The more one is hated, I find, the happier one is.'
– LOUIS-FERDINAND CÉLINE

'Happiness is a warm gun.'
– LENNON AND McCARTNEY, song title

HEALTH

'Never go to a doctor whose office plants have died.'
– ERMA BOMBECK

'I took, early in the morning, a good dose of Elizir, and

hung three spiders about my neck, and they drove my acne
away – *Deo gratias.*'   – ELIAS ASHMOLE

'If God wanted us to bend over he'd put diamonds on the
floor.'   – JOAN RIVERS

'I'm a fat anorexic.'   – KIRI TE KANAWA

'The head anointed with the juice of leeks preserveth the
hair from falling out. A mouse roasted and given to children to eat remedieth pissing the bed.'
                                     – *The Widdowes Treasure* (1595)

'I started smoking during the war. I have kept it up ever
since. It keeps me healthy.'   – MARLENE DIETRICH

'Cleanliness is almost as bad as godliness.'
                                               – SAMUEL BUTLER

'Crabs are beautiful.'   – DONOVAN

HEAVEN

'There is no reason to think that there will be pianos in the
next world.'   – *The Universe*

'I don't think there is sex in heaven. If people only want to
go to heaven for sex, they'd better have heaven on earth.'
                                               – BILLY GRAHAM

'Don't wait for pie in the sky when you die! Get yours now, with ice cream on top!'
– FREDERICK J. EIKERENKOETTER II,
'The Reverend Ike'

HISTORY

'History is a set of lies agreed upon.'   – NAPOLEON

'History is an account, mostly false, of events, mostly unimportant, which are brought about by rulers, mostly knaves, and soldiers, mostly fools.'   – AMBROSE BIERCE

'History repeats itself. Historians repeat each other.'
– PHILIP GUADALLA

'We have wasted History like a bunch of drunks shooting dice back in the men's crapper of the local bar.'
– CHARLES BUKOWSKI

'The people who are always hankering loudest for some golden yesteryear usually drive new cars.'
– RUSSELL BAKER

'History doesn't pass the dishes again.'
– LOUIS FERDINAND CÉLINE

HONESTY

'Honesty: The most important thing in life. Unless you really know how to fake it, you'll never make it.'

— BERNARD ROSENBERG

'The louder he talked of his honor, the faster we counted our spoons.'

— RALPH WALDO EMERSON

HYPE

'Brian Aldiss . . . is Joyce, Huxley, Waugh, on a pot party, with Arthur C. Clarke trying to give a lecture to Isaac Asimov while Noël Coward sings and plays the piano.'

— Publisher's blurb

'Adolf Hitler was one of the first rock stars . . . I think he was quite as good as Jagger. It's astounding. When he hit that stage, he worked an audience. Good God! He was no politician. He was a media artist himself. He use politics and theatrics and created this thing that governed and controlled the show for those twelve years. The world will never see his like. He staged a country.'   — DAVID BOWIE

JOURNALISM

'The press are good guys. They are helpful with their questions.'

— RICHARD NIXON

'People don't actually read newspapers. They get into them every morning, like a hot bath.'   – MARSHALL McLUHAN

'You should always believe all you read in the newspapers, as this makes them more interesting.'   – ROSE MACAULEY

'The lowest depth to which people can sink before God is defined by the word "journalist". If I was a father and had a daughter who was seduced I should not despair over her; I would hope for her salvation. But if I had a son who became a journalist, and continued to be one for five years, I would give him up.'   – SOREN KIERKEGAARD

'Rock journalism is people who can't write interviewing people who can't talk for people who can't read.'
    – FRANK ZAPPA

'B-52 bomber found on the moon.'
    – Headline in *Sunday Sport*

'We derive our inspiration from God, but we are grateful to *The Times* for the strengthening of our convictions.'
    – BISHOP OF CARLISLE

'Your front page article about Africans being shot made me feel sick. Could not this kind of story be condensed and made more pleasant?'   – Letter to *Daily Mirror*

LAW

'I do not know whether you are a knave or a fool if you thought you were going to corrupt a police officer with a paltry £5.'   – MR HERBERT METCALFE
magistrate

'This form was drawn up in 1936, and it does not clearly state what is meant. It is just a legal document.'
– *Daily Mirror*

'It is the very merit of the death penalty that its bark is worse than its bite.'   – LORD QUICKSWOOD,
Letter in the *Daily Telegraph*

'A person guilty of rape should be castrated. That would stop him pretty quick.'   – BILLY GRAHAM

'Judge: A law student who marks his own examination papers.'   – H. L. MENCKEN

'When you have no basis for an argument, abuse the plaintiff.'   – CICERO

'The first thing we do, let's kill all the lawyers.'
– SHAKESPEARE, *Henry VI, Part II*

LIES

'Any fool can tell the truth, but it requires a man of some sense to know how to lie well.'　　– SAMUEL BUTLER

'Martin Luther King is the most notorious liar in the country.'　　– J. EDGAR HOOVER

'I have always loved truth so passionately that I have often resorted to lying as a way of introducing it into minds which were ignorant of its charms.'　　– CASANOVA

'You don't tell deliberate lies, but sometimes you have to be evasive.'　　– MARGARET THATCHER

'We fulfil our norms, our principles. What we say is always the truth. If someone wants to doubt this truth, he should do so, but we will never allow someone to try to test our realities or to refute our truths.'　　– FIDEL CASTRO,
on why Cuba did not allow the
International Red Cross to visit its prisons.

'If the Republicans will stop telling lies about the Democrats, we will stop telling the truth about them.'
– ADLAI STEVENSON

'If I took my sunglasses off, everyone could see that I was lying through my teeth.'　　– GEORGE MICHAEL

LIFE

'Life is one long process of getting tired.'   – SAMUEL BUTLER

'Millions long for immortality who do not know what to do with themselves on a rainy Sunday afternoon.'
                                                        – SUSAN ERTZ

'Not a shred of evidence exists in favour of the idea that life is serious.'   – BRENDAN GILL

'Most of the evils of life arise from man's inability to sit still in a room.'   – BLAISE PASCAL

'How I hate the attitude of ordinary people to life. How I loathe ordinariness! How from my soul I abhor nice simple people, with their eternal price-list. It makes my blood boil.'   – D. H. LAWRENCE

'First you dream, then you die.'   – CORNELL WOOLRICH

'I didn't know how babies were made until I was pregnant with my fourth child five years later.'   – LORETTA LYNN,
                                                who married at age thirteen

'All I want from life is plenty of booze, plenty of women, and as many drugs I can take. And somewhere to live while I'm doing it.'   – RAT SCABIES
                                                        The Damned

'I don't wanna take no year's sabbatical and go see some guru in the Himalayas to learn the secret of life. I don't think there's too many secrets to life, really.'

– CHARLIE DANIELS

'Thirty seconds after you're born, you have a past; sixty seconds after, you start lying to yourself about it.'

– DAVID CRONENBERG
The Brood

'A man with a career can have no time to waste upon his wife and friends; he has to devote it wholly to his enemies.'

– JOHN OLIVER HOBBES

'Whatever else we are intended to do, we are not intended to succeed: failure is the fate allotted.'

– ROBERT LOUIS STEVENSON

'Consultants are people who borrow your watch and tell you what time it is, then walk off with the watch.'

– ROBERT TOWNSEND

'Have you noticed that life, real honest to goodness life, with murders and catastrophes and fabulous inheritances, happens almost exclusively in the newspapers?'

– JEAN ANOUILH

'You should make a point of trying every experience once, except incest and folk-dancing.'   – Anon. (19th century)

'Truth is something somehow discreditable to someone.'

– H. H. MENCKEN

'I think the human body's one of the most ugly things ever created.'   – JOHN LYDON, Public Image Limited

'You gotta keep changing. Shirts, old ladies, whatever.'
                                                        – NEIL YOUNG

'I have life *dicked*.'   – TED NUGENT

LOVE

'Love is what you feel for a dog or a pussy cat. It doesn't apply to humans . . .'   – JOHNNY ROTTEN

'She was twenty years younger than I was, and at forty-six or thereabouts one begins to feel that one's time for love is over; one is consultant rather than practitioner.'
                                                – GEORGE MOORE (1914)

'When people are in love, they are in a magnetic state, and are very much astonished at themselves when they come to their senses. The other night the man who caused me more good and evil feelings than I ever knew before or since the three years his influence lasted, called here. I am frightened when I think of the last year, and yet even that one is now like a tale I have read – has no more to do with me, my present me, than the woes of Dido! Well, as I said, that very man came in the other evening, and stayed some time; he really is the most prosy, wearisome, commonplace person nature ever created. Once, and not so long ago, that **hour would have gilded a week; and now it required an** effort of politeness not to give an intelligible hint to shorten his visit!'   – GERALDINE JEWSBURY (1843)

'Don't threaten me with love, baby. Let's just go walking in the rain.'   – BILLIE HOLIDAY

'Before you love, learn to run through snow leaving no footprints.'   – TURKISH PROVERB

'Any time that is not spent on love is wasted.'   – TASSO

'Love is a kind of warfare.'   – OVID

'Lovers' vows do not reach the ears of the gods.'
                                                   – CALLIMACHUS

'A voice from a jar of vaseline. This too is love.'
                                                   – GAVIN EWART

'Love: the delusion that one woman differs from another.'
                                                   – H. L. MENCKEN

'All they that loved not tobacco and boys were fools.'
                                             – CHRISTOPHER MARLOWE

'No matter how much a woman loves a man, it would still give her a glow to see him commit suicide for her.'
                                                   – H. L. MENCKEN

'The first kiss is stolen by the man; the last is begged by the woman.'
– H. L. MENCKEN

'Adultery is the application of democracy to love.'
– H. L. MENCKEN

'If two people love each other there can be no happy end to it.'
– ERNEST HEMINGWAY

MANKIND

'The human race, to which so many of my readers belong . . .'
– G. K. CHESTERTON

'Such is the human race, often it seems a pity that Noah . . . didn't miss the boat.'
– MARK TWAIN

'Individually, men may present a more or less rational appearance, eating, sleeping and scheming. But humanity as a whole is changeful, mystical, fickle, delightful. Men are men but Man is a woman.'
– G. K. CHESTERTON

'The more I see of men, the more I like dogs.'
– MADAME DE STAËL

MARRIAGE

'I married beneath me. All women do.'
– NANCY ASTOR

'I feel sure that no girl could go to the altar, and would probably *refuse*, if she knew *all* . . .   – QUEEN VICTORIA

'I'm reading Sydney Smith – his life – with only one wish in the world: that I'd married him.'   – VIRGINIA WOOLF

'Mr Solus: Now I think marriage is an excellent remedy for the spleen. I have known a gentleman at a feast receive an affront, disguise his rage, step home, vent it all upon his wife, return to his companions, and be as good company as if nothing had happened.'   – From a play by MRS INCHBALD

'I'd marry again if I found a man who had $15,000,000, would sign over half of it to me before the marriage, and guarantee he'd be dead within a year.'   – BETTE DAVIS

' . . . the trewith is, though he naturally loved the company of woemen, yett he was allwayes naturally averse to mariage, and some times, dreaminge he was maried, haith wept in his sleep very much.'   – ANON. (1668)

'I don't think matrimony consistent with the liberty of the subject.'   – FARQUHAR

'I've been married six months. She looks like a million dollars, but she only knows a hundred and twenty words and she's only got two ideas in her head. The other one's hats.'   – ART LINKLETTER, *Don Juan in America*

'A married man will do anything for money.'
– TALLEYRAND

'Marriage is the only war where one sleeps with the enemy.'
— Mexican proverb

'Why the hell should I get a wife when the man next door's got one?'
— FURRY LEWIS, 87-year-old blues artist

'Marriage: the only adventure open to the cowardly.'
— VOLTAIRE

'When a man steals your wife, there is no better revenge than to let him keep her.'
— SACHA GUITRY

'A husband should not insult his wife publicly, at parties. He should insult her in the privacy of the home.'
— JAMES THURBER

'It destroys one's nerves to be amiable every day to the same human being.'
— BENJAMIN DISRAELI

'Once you are married there is nothing left for you, not even suicide, but to be good.'
— ROBERT LOUIS STEVENSON

'Mr Commissioner Bush James, in the Divorce Court today, remarked: "For a husband to permit his wife to go on committing adultery and then to go into the next room and himself commit adultery with his hostess seems to me an extraordinary piece of bad behaviour." '
— *Evening Argus*

' "People," he commented, "don't hang from their bed-room windows late at night, screaming for some considerable time, because they cannot have relations with their wives." He thought it had been proved that this was what Mr W-- had done.'

– News of the World

'When two people marry, they become in the eyes of the law one person, and that person is the husband.'

– SHANE ALEXANDER

'A man in love is incomplete until he has married. Then he's finished.'

– ZSA ZSA GABOR

'It is one thing for a woman to have her face smacked from time to time and be punched in the normal wear and tear of married life, and quite another thing to have her face smacked and punched by a man who hates her.'

– Court report in *Evening Standard*

'The great use of female beauty, the great practical advantage of it is, that it naturally and unavoidably tends to keep the husband in good humour with himself, to make him, to use the dealer's phrase, pleased with his bargain.'

– WILLIAM COBBETT

'The trouble with marrying your mistress is that you create a job vacancy.'

– SIR JAMES GOLDSMITH

'All my wives live in Wiltshire.'

– Overheard at Longchamps

MEN

'Every man needs a resonance. A woman who loves a man should be content to be just that.'   – MARLENE DIETRICH

'I actually can't think of anything more aggressive than actually sticking something into someone.'
    – GRAHAM HILL,
arguing that women are not aggressive
enough to challenge male drivers.

'Y'know the problem with men? After the birth, we're irrelevant.   – DUSTIN HOFFMAN

'A hard man is good to find.'   – MAE WEST

'All real men love to eat.'   – MARLENE DIETRICH

'The difference between a moral man and a man of honor is that the latter regrets a discreditable act, even when it has worked and he has not been caught.'   – H. L. MENCKEN

'A gentleman is one who never strikes a woman without provocation.'   – H. L. MENCKEN

'Men have a much better time of it than women. For one thing they marry later. For another thing, they die earlier.'
    – H. L. MENCKEN

'I like men to behave like men – strong and childish.'
    – FRANÇOISE SAGAN

'I want a man who's kind and understanding. Is that too much to ask of a millionaire?'　　– ZSA ZSA GABOR

'All men are led by one thing, and that's their willy.'
– SHIRLIE, of Pepsi and Shirlie

MILITARY/DEFENSE

'How did I know the B-1 bomber was an airplane? I thought it was vitamins for the troops.'
– RONALD REAGAN

'I don't think there'll be a war. The Führer doesn't want his new buildings bombed.'　　– UNITY MITFORD (1938)

'The United States has much to offer the third world war.'
– RONALD REAGAN

'My fellow Americans, I am pleased to tell you I just signed legislation that will outlaw Russia forever. We begin bombing in five minutes.'　　– RONALD REAGAN,
in rehearsal for broadcast,
subsequently aired.

'We are not interested in the possibilities of defeat. They do not exist.'　　– QUEEN VICTORIA,
on the Boer War

'The atomic bomb will not go off – and I speak as an expert in explosives.'　　– ADMIRAL W. LEAHY
to President Truman (1945)

'The best defence against the atom bomb is not to be there when it goes off.'
— *British Army Journal* (1949)

'They're asking women to do impossible things. I don't believe women can carry a pack, live in a foxhole, or go a week without a bath.'
— GENERAL WILLIAM WESTMORELAND

'It is necessary for technical reasons that these warheads should be stored with the top at the bottom, and the bottom at the top. In order that there may be no doubt as to which is the top and which is the bottom, for storage purposes, it will be seen that the bottom of each head has been labelled with the word TOP.'
— Admiralty instruction dealing with the storage of warheads or torpedoes

'Even in the age of nuclear warfare the best training for an officer is to ride a horse. It brings out the best qualities in a chap.'
— Army Captain quoted in *News Chronicle*

'The snowdrop is more powerful than the Panzer.'
— BEVERLEY NICHOLS

'As soon as you know an H-bomb is on the way, run out and paint your windows with a mixture of whitewash and curdled milk to deflect dangerous rays. Soak your curtains and upholstery with a solution of borax and starch to prevent fire.'
— Lecturer in civil defence reported in **Reynolds News**

'The first Californian prunes, part of £2,000,000 worth of fruit to be exchanged for US rocket bases in Britain, have just arrived in this country.   – *Daily Express*

'If you want to safeguard your children against atomic radiation and fall-out, take them to Brighton's sea-front cliffs, and let them eat chalk.'   – Physicist quoted in *Brighton Evening News*

'There is a simple answer to the atomic bomb. It is that no weapon has ever been invented for which the answer doesn't exist.'   – BRIGADIER A. M. TOYE, VC, MC

'I have to have no fear of atomic bombs. A good six-inch wall is sufficient protection against any atom bomb, as it was against bombs during the recent war, providing that you are not too near to it, of course.'

– CAPTAIN HARRY WARD, MC

'Cogito ergo boom.'   – SUSAN SONTAG

MONEY

'If you would know what the Lord God thinks of money, you have only to look at those to whom he gives it.'

– MAURICE BARING

'Those who set out to serve both God and Mammon soon discover there is no God.'   – LOGAN PEARSALL SMITH, *Afterthoughts*

'In all likelihood, world inflation is over.'
> – Managing Director of International
> Monetary Fund (1959)

'I'm glad to know there are rich people around. It affects me like looking at sunsets, and snow-capped mountains.'
> – ENOCH POWELL

'Money makes a man laugh.'   – JOHN SELDEN

'It's a full-time job just trying to decide how to spend all this money.'   – ARTHUR C. CLARKE

'Those who have some means think that the most important thing in the world is love. The poor know that it is money.'   – GERALD BRENAN

'It is only the poor who are forbidden to beg.'
> – ANATOLE FRANCE

'I think every young man should have a hobby. Learning to handle money is the best hobby.'   – JACK HURLEY

'Seek wealth, it's good.'   – IVAN BOESKY

MORALITY

'Nothing is illegal if a hundred businessmen decide to do it, and that's true anywhere in the world.'   – ANDREW YOUNG

'Whether Queen Elizabeth sleeps with Prince Philip or not is her affair. I think that if you swing with chickens, that is your perfect right.'   – LIBERACE

'A hand on your cock is more moral – and more fun – than a finger on the trigger.'   – LAWRENCE LIPTON,
Radio Free America column,
Los Angeles Free Press

'Cannibals have the same notions of right and wrong that we have. They make war in the same anger and passion that move us, and the same crimes are committed everywhere. Eating fallen enemies is only an extra ceremonial. The wrong does not consist in roasting them, but in killing them.'   – VOLTAIRE

'Don't call a man honest just because he never had the chance to steal.'   – Yiddish saying

'When choosing between two evils, I always like to try the one I've never tried before.'   – MAE WEST

'First secure an independent income, then practice virtue.'   – Greek proverb

'Moral indignation is jealousy with a halo.'   – H. G. WELLS

'What are we faced with in the nineteenth century? An age where woman was sacred; and where you could buy a thirteen-year-old girl for a few pounds . . . if you wanted her for only an hour or two . . . where more churches were built than in the whole previous history of the country; and where one in sixty houses in London was a brothel . . . where it was universally maintained that women do not have orgasms; and yet every prostitute was taught to simulate them. Where there was an enormous progress and liberation in every other field of human activity; and nothing but tyranny in the most personal and fundamental.'

– JOHN FOWLES
on 'Victorian Values'

'It is not my mode of thought that has caused my misfortunes, but the mode of thought of others.'

– MARQUIS DE SADE
(1749–1814)

'Conscience is the inner voice which warns us that someone may be looking.'
– H. L. MENCKEN

MOVIES

'Movies are fun, but they're not a cure for cancer.'
– WARREN BEATTY

'Paint eyeballs on my eyelids and I'll sleepwalk through any picture.'
– ROBERT MITCHUM
estimate of his own acting

'If my fanny squirms, it's bad. If my fanny doesn't squirm, it's good. It's as simple as that.'
– HARRY COHN
Columbia boss

'I didn't know the whole world was wired to Harry Cohn's ass.'
    – HERMAN MANKIEWICZ
    on the fanny test

'I fall in love with all the actors in my films. They are the prolongations of my penis. Yes, my penis, like Pinocchio's nose, my penis grows!'
    – BERNARD BEROLUCCI
    Director

'An actor's a guy who, if you ain't talking about him, ain't listening.'
    MARLON BRANDO

'They shot too many pictures and not enough actors.'
    – WALTER WINCHELL

'To me, bad taste is what entertainment is all about.'
    – JOHN WATERS

'If you love horror movies, you've got to have a love for pure *shit*.'
    – STEPHEN KING

'Always make the audience suffer as much as possible.'
    – ALFRED HITCHCOCK

'I guess I didn't throw enough Christians to the lions.'
    – JOHN BOORMAN,
    explaining the failure of *Exorcist II*

'You can't find closeness in Hollywood. Everyone does the fake closeness so well.'
    – CARRIE FISHER

MUSIC

'Oh how wonderful, really wonderful, opera would be if there were no singers!' – ROSSINI

'Madonna is so hairy, when she lifted her arm I thought it was Tina Turner in her armpit.' – JOAN RIVERS

'There are no woman composers, never have been and possibly never will be.' – SIR THOMAS BEECHAM

'I don't know anything about music – in my line you don't have to.' – ELVIS PRESLEY

'All my records are comedy records.' – BOB DYLAN

'I'd rather be dead than singing "Satisfaction" when I'm forty-five.' – MICK JAGGER

'A vile beastly rottenheaded foolbegotten brazenthroated pernicious piggish screaming, tearing, roaring, perplexing, splitmecrackle crashmecriggle insane ass of a woman is practising, howling below-stairs with a brute of a singing-master so horribly, that my head is nearly off.' – EDWARD LEAR (1859)

'You should never trust anyone who listens to Mahler before they're 40.' – CLIVE JAMES

'The sound of a harpsichord – two skeletons copulating on a tin roof in a thunderstorm.'   – SIR THOMAS BEECHAM

'We don't want to censor your songs. What we want to do is change your song. You're the younger generation; you believe in change.'   – ROICCO LAGINESTRA,
RCA Records President,
quoted by Paul Kantner

'Rock and Roll is a communicable disease.'
– *New York Times* (1956)

'I like Beethoven, especially the poems.'   – RINGO STARR

'Rock and Roll is phony and false and sung, written and played for the most part by cretinous goons.'
– FRANK SINATRA

'Music helps not the toothache.'   – GEORGE HERBERT

'I love Wagner, but the music I prefer is that of a cat hung up by its tail outside a window and trying to stick to the panes of glass with its claws.'   – CHARLES BAUDELAIRE

'Rock music is the most brutal, ugly, vicious form of expression . . . sly, lewd – in plain fact, dirty . . . (a) rancid-smelling aphrodisiac . . . martial music of every delinquent on the face of the earth.'   – FRANK SINATRA
in the *New York Times*, (1957)

'My songs only exist in the essence of silence.'   – DONOVAN

'When you're making records for America, you're making records for a market whose mentality is ten years behind the rest of the world.'   – MIKE CHAPMAN

'When an individual with as much perception as myself decides to honor those pipsqueaks by recording them instead of pissing on them, the first thing they should do is kneel and kiss his ass.'   – DOUG WESTON,
owner of Los Angeles Troubadour Club,
accused of taping bands without their permission

'Why does that pompous creep come off bad-mouthing me like that when he never even met me and probably hasn't even seen my act? . . . Just for that I'm gonna stick around in this business just long enough to piss on John Denver's flowers!   – ALICE COOPER,
replying to John Denver's assertion that he
would be around when Alice was long forgotton

'If this doesn't put the cunt back in country, I don't know what will.'   – CARLENE CARTER,
introducing 'Swap-Meat Rag'

'I refused to write the music for "Plaistow Patricia" as I didn't really get off on the words. I thought any song that starts off "Arseholes, bastards, fucking cunts and pricks" is not exactly going to be a major No. 1 world hit.'
                                    – CHAS JANKEL

'Men compose symphonies. Women compose babies.'
                                    – *Time* magazine

'You can never get a woman to sit down and listen to a drum solo.'   – CLIVE JAMES

'These boys won't make it. Four groups are out. Go back to Liverpool, Mr Epstein – you have a good busines there.'
                                              – Decca record company,
                                              about The Beatles (1962)

'I declare that the Beatles are mutants. Prototypes of evolutionary agents sent by God endowed with a mysterious power to create a new human species – a young race of laughing freemen.'   – TIMOTHY LEARY

'I didn't change my name in honor of Dylan Thomas. That's just a story. I've done more for Dylan Thomas than he's done for me. Look how many kids . . .'   – BOB DYLAN

'A musicologist is a man who can read music but can't hear it.'   – SIR THOMAS BEECHAM

'I like to think of us as Clearasil on the face of the nation. Jim Morrison would have said that if he was smart, but he's dead.'   – LOU REED,
                                              on his band's tour

'I believe rock can do anything – it's the ultimate vehicle for everything. It's the ultimate vehicle for saying anything, for putting down anything, for building up anything, for killing and creating. It's the absolute ultimate vehicle for self-destruction, which is the most incredible thing, because there's nothing as effective as that – not in terms of art, anyway, or what we call art. You just can't be as effectively self-destructive if you're a writer, for example, or a painter; you just can't make sure that you're never going to fucking raise your head again. Whereas if you're a rock star you really can.'   – PETE TOWNSHEND

'Do you think Paul McCartney makes records just to annoy me personally, or does he want to get up everyone's fucking nose with his fucking antics?'   – ALEX HARVEY

'We go home safe in the knowledge that we've deafened a few.'   – PHIL TAYLOR, Motorhead

'I'm interested in concepts and philosophies. I am not interested in wallpaper, which most music is.'
    – JOHN LENNON

'It's a bit like having an orgasm. Sometimes an orgasm is better than being onstage; sometimes being onstage is better than having an orgasm.'   – MICK JAGGER,
    on his work

'We're thinking of learning a new chord. That's our project for the year.'   – JOHN SPARKS,
    Dr Feelgood

'Leonardo had the Medici family, we've got EMI to look after us!'   – JOHN,
    Duran Duran

'Jagger is rather like Dostoevsky's Brother Karamazov who, when told by his venerable brother that pain must exist so that we might learn of goodness, replied that if it was necessary that one small child should suffer in order that he should be made more aware, he did not deny the existence of God, but merely respectfully returned his ticket of admission to Heaven.

That is Mick Jagger's kind of rebellion.'

– KEITH ALTHAM,
Melody Maker

'Mick Jagger is about as sexy as a pissing toad.'

– TRUMAN CAPOTE

OPERA

'Opera is when a guy gets stabbed in the back and instead of bleeding, he sings.'

– ED GARDNER

'Going to the opera, like getting drunk, is a sin that carries its own punishment with it – and that is a very serious one.'

– HANNAH MORE (1775)

'One goes to see a tragedy to be moved, to the opera one goes either for want of any other interest or to facilitate digestion.'

– VOLTAIRE

'Is Wagner a human being at all? Is he not really a disease?'

– FRIEDRICH NIETZCHE

PATRIOTISM

'A nation is a society united by delusions about its ancestry and by common hatred of its neighbours.' – DEAN INGE

'The rich are setting us a very good example. They knew that in supporting us in this way they were signing their own death-warrants. They have lost almost all of their incomes. They have completely altered their way of living, and have been driven from their beloved homes.

'These unexampled sacrifices they have borne without a murmur for the sake of their country.' – DEAN INGE, in *Evening Standard*

'Mr Jones, landlord of the 300-year-old Rose and Crown, said: "One Belgian tried to strangle me. I did not mind him at my throat, but I took exception to a drunken foreigner grabbing my precious 1st Airborne Division tie." ' – *Daily Mirror*

'America has never been defeated in the proud 190-year history of this country, and we shall not be defeated by Vietnam.' – RICHARD NIXON

PHILOSOPHY

'There usually is an answer to any problem: simple, clean and wrong.' – H. L. MENCKEN

'Never contend with a man who has nothing to lose.'
– GRACIAN

'The best way to keep one's word is not to give it.'
– Napoleon

'The more I read him, the less I wonder that they poisoned him.'   – MACAULEY, on Socrates

'To a man who is afraid everything rustles.'   – SOPHOCLES

'The optimist proclaims that we live in the best of all possible worlds, and the pessimist fears this is true.'
– JAMES BRANCH CABELL

'I don't think about deep things – if you can't take a bite of it, it doesn't exist.'   – TED NUGENT

POETS AND POETRY

'I used to read Browning with interest and respect, if not with pleasure, until one afternoon I saw him running after an omnibus at the end of Piccadilly; and I could not stand his loftier poetry after that.'   – CECIL TORR

'It seems to me that a sonnet is the utmost length to which a rhymed poem should extend.'   – SAMUEL BUTLER

'A poet in history is divine, but a poet in the next room is a joke.'
                                                      – MAX EASTMAN

'Poetry is a synthesis of hyacinths and biscuits.'
                                                      – CARL SANDBERG

POLITICS

'Don't tell my mother I'm in politics – she thinks I play piano in a whorehouse.'   – A saying, *c.* 1930

'A politician is a person with whose politics you don't agree; if you agree with him he is a statesman.'
                                                      – DAVID LLOYD GEORGE

'Whenever I get a train of thought started someone wants me to stop and glorify National Pickle Week.'
                                                      – SPIRO AGNEW

'A Nixon–Agnew Administration will abolish the credibility gap and re-establish the truth – the whole truth – as its policy.'   – SPIRO AGNEW

'After all, what does a politician have but credibility?'
                                                      – SPIRO AGNEW

'Ayatollah Khomeini will one day be viewed as some kind of saint.'
                                                      – ANDREW YOUNG,
                                                      US Ambassador to the UN (1976)

'I know I am going to be President.' – SENATOR GARY HART

'I've talked to you on a number of occasions about the economic problems our nation faces, and I am prepared to tell you it's in a hell of a mess . . . We're not connected to the press room yet, are we?' – RONALD REAGAN

'When more and more people are thrown out of work unemployment results.' – CALVIN COOLIDGE

'I don't believe the Poles consider themselves dominated by the Soviet Union.' – GERALD FORD

'I'm glad I'm not Brezhnev. Being the Russian leader in the Kremlin, you never know if someone's tape-recording what you say.' – RICHARD NIXON

'All political parties die of swallowing their own lies.'
– JONATHAN SWIFT,
Thoughts on Various Subjects

'In politics there is no honour.' – BENJAMIN DISRAELI,
Vivian Grey

'An honest politician is one who, when he is bought, will stay bought.' – SIMON CAMERON,
(19th-century US politician)

'How can anyone govern a country that has 246 different kinds of cheese?' – CHARLES DE GAULLE

'As far as socialism means anything, it must be about the wider distribution of smoked salmon and caviar.'

– LORD MARCH

'The function of socialism is to raise suffering to a higher level.'

– NORMAL MAILER

'If you've got 'em by the balls, their hearts and minds will follow.'

– sign in the White House office of
Charles Colson, aide to President Nixon

'Now that I've won, I'm gonna make Attila the Hun look like a faggot!'

– FRANK RIZZO,
on being re-elected Mayor of Philadelphia

'If you want to find a politician free of any influence, you can find Adolph Hitler, who made up his own mind.'

– EUGENE McCARTHY

'People ask me who my heroes are. I have only one – Hitler. I admire Hitler because he pulled his country together when it was in a terrible state in the early thirties. But the situation here is so desperate now that one man would not be enough. We need four or five Hitlers in Vietnam.'

– NGUYEN CAO KY,
Premier of South Vietnam (1965)

'There are some politicians who, if their constituents were cannibals, would promise them missionaries for dinner.'

– H. L. MENCKEN

'I've got what it takes to stay.'

– RICHARD NIXON

'The whole nation loves him, because it feels safe in his hands, like a child in the arms of his mother.'

– JOSEPH GOEBBELS,
on Adolf Hitler

'Every President needs his son-of-a-bitch; I'm Nixon's.'

– BOB HALDEMAN,
Chief of Staff to President Nixon

'All my life I have suffered from very hairy ears. Two years ago a friend told me that this was because I was a Liberal . . . This so impressed me that I joined the Socialist Party, and now I have very hairy backs to my hands too.'

– Letter in *Daily Mail*

'It is my hope, and I believe, that under the new system of guarantees the new Czechoslovakia will find greater security than she has ever enjoyed in the past.'

– NEVILE CHAMBERLAIN,
quoted in *Times Education Supplement*

'A flea can be taught everything a congressman can.'

– MARK TWAIN

'Being in politics is like being a football coach. You have to be smart enough to understand the game and dumb enough to think it important.'
– EUGENE McCARTHY

'There's a sexual revolution going on, and I think that with our current foreign policy, we'll probably be sending troops in there any minute to break it up.'   – MEL BROOKS

'If it takes a blood-bath, let's get it over with. No more appeasement.'   – RONALD REAGAN (1970)

'No one in his right mind would make such a statement.'
                          – Ronal Reagan's Press Secretary (1970)

'We shall reach greater and greater platitudes of achievement.'   – MAYOR RICHARD J. DALEY

'There is no housing shortage in Lincoln today – just a rumour that is put about by people who have nowhere to live.'   – CLLR MRS G. L. MURFIN
                          Mayor of Lincoln, in the *Lincolnshire Echo*

'Bad officials are elected by good citizens who do not vote.'
                          – GEORGE JEAN NATHAN

'Under capitalism man exploits man; under socialism the reverse is true.'   – Polish proverb

'The oppressed are allowed once every few years to decide which particular representatives of the oppressing class are to represent and repress them.   – KARL MARX

'The rights you have are the rights given to you by this Committee [House Un-American Activities Committee]. *We* will determine what rights you have and what rights you have not got.'   – J. PARNELL THOMAS

'The mind of the universe is communistic.'
                          – MARCUS AURELIUS

'Fascist rule prevents worse injustice, and if Fascism goes under, nothing can save the country from chaos: God's cause goes under with it.'   – ARTHUR, CARDINAL HINSLEY

'Einstein's theory of relativity, as practiced by Congressmen, simply means getting members of your family on the payroll.'   – JAMES H. BOREN

'Only a fool wants a confrontation, and only a fool wants a strike.'   – ARTHUR SCARGILL

'The tree of liberty must be refreshed from time to time with the blood of patriots and tyrants. It is its natural manure.'   – THOMAS JEFFERSON (1743–1826)

'Let us begin by committing ourselves to the truth, to see it like it is and to tell it like it is, to find the truth, to speak the truth and to live with the truth. That's what we'll do.
    – RICHARD NIXON
    Republican nomination acceptance
    speech, Miami, August 1968

'Voters quickly forget what a man says.'   – RICHARD NIXON

'The White House has no involvement in this particular incident.'   – White House press conference,
    on the Watergate break-in, June 1972

'When the President does it, that means that it is not illegal.'
    – RICHARD NIXON

'One of the shallowest disdains is the sneer against the professional politician.'   – JUSTICE FELIX FRANKFURTER

'We believe that a centre party would have no roots, no principles, no philosophy and no values.'
– SHIRLEY WILLIAMS, 1980

'We're going to move left and right at the same time.'
– GOVERNOR JERRY BROWN

'I have the thermometer in my mouth and I am listening to it all the time.'   – WILLIAM WHITELAW

'I don't blame anyone, except perhaps all of us.'
– WILLIAM WHITELAW

'No woman in my time will be Prime Minister or Foreign Secretary – not the top jobs. Anyway, I wouldn't want to be Prime Minister. You have to give yourself one hundred per cent.   – MARGARET THATCHER,
(October 1969)

'I am willing to take your affairs in hand, but not into my liver and lungs.'   – MONTAIGNE,
when he was elected Mayor of Bordeaux

'Traditional parliamentary democracies are among the most tyrannical dictatorships the world has ever known.'
– COLONEL GADDAFI,
The Green Book

'Now I know what a statesman is; he's a dead politician. We need more statesmen.'
– BOB EDWARDS

'Political ability is the ability to foretell what is going to happen tomorrow, next week, next month and next year. And to have the ability afterwards to explain why it didn't happen.'
– WINSTON CHURCHILL

'Politicians make strange bedfellows, but they all share the same bunk.'
– EDGAR A. SHOAFF

'Politicians are the same all over. They promise to build a bridge even when there is no river.' – NIKITA KHRUSHCHEV

'I ask you to join me in a toast to President Figueiredo and the people of Bolivia . . . no, that's where I'm going.'
– RONALD REAGAN,
in Brazil, before going to Bogota,
Columbia (December 1982)

'I'd like to extend a warm welcome to Chairman Mo.'
– RONALD REAGAN,
To President Doe of Liberia

'Balancing your budget is like protecting your virtue – you have to learn to say no.'
– RONALD REAGAN
(January 1980)

'If President's don't do it to their wives, they do it to the country.'
– MEL BROOKS

POWER

'Power is like a woman you want to stay in bed with for ever.'
                                                    – PATRICK ANDERSON

'Women are always attracted to power. I do not think there could ever be a conqueror so bloody that most women would not willingly lie with him in the hope of bearing a son who would be every bit as ferocious as the father.'
                                                    – GORE VIDAL

'Being powerful is like being a lady. If you have to tell people you are, you ain't.'
                                            – JESSE CARR, Union leader

'By and large, the editors will have complete freedom, as long as they agree with the policy I have laid down.'
                                    – VICTOR MATHEWS, newspaper proprietor

'You can get much further with a kind word and a gun than you can with a kind word alone.'
                                                    – AL CAPONE

PSYCHIATRY AND PSYCHOLOGY

'Psychoanalysis is the illness whose cure it considers itself to be.'
                                                    – KARL KRAUS

'I got a momma who joined the Peace Corps when she was 68. I got one sister who's a Holy Roller preacher. Another wears a helmet and rides a motor cycle. And my brother

thinks he's going to be President. So that makes me the
only sane one in the family.'   – BILLY CARTER

'Behavioral psychology is the science of pulling habits out
of rats.'   – DR DOUGLAS BUSCH

'We are all born mad. Some remain so.'   – SAMUEL BECKETT

RACE

'Few people can be happy unless they hate some other
person, nation or creed.'   – BERTRAND RUSSELL

'The native black population is so unimportant that
beyond mentioning them and pointing out to the children
that their civilization is that of the Stone Age, and that it is
impossible to raise them to ours, it is wise to ignore them.
Children are inclined to think that the black people of
Australia are as important as the black people of Africa.'
                                            – *Teacher's World*

'I'll tell you what the coloureds want. It's three things:
first, a tight pussy; second, loose shoes, and third, a warm
place to shit. That's all!'   – EARL BUTZ,
                                       Secretary of Agriculture (1976)

'In extreme cases marijuana can so destroy a man's charac-
ter that he mixes freely with persons of another race.'
                              – South African textbook on Criminology

'I cannot help wondering why God created coloured people, seeing the resultant difficulties caused thereby.'

– The Church Times

'The sexual habits of the Pakistanis arouse a variety of interesting comments, some of which reveal as much about local mores as about the immigrants. One young woman I met in Bradford said they had all kinds of perverted customs: they even made *the women* take off their clothes before sexual intercourse.'

– The Observer

'When a white man laughs he means his laughter and regulates it. With the black race the contrary is the case. Both coal-black mammy and her male counterpart when they are tickled laugh too much, partly out of vanity and because of their superb teeth, and partly out of a mentality which when fully grown retains much of the child. That is why, when both must inhabit the same country, it is necessary for the whites to look after and care for the black.'

– JAMES AGATE

'It's great when they're little piccaninnies; they're cute and everbody's a do-gooder. But what about when they're older . . . fourteen or fifteen?'

– WILLIAM POTTER, a Pennsylvania judge, ruling non-white children could not be adopted by white parents

'Everybody's coloured or else you wouldn't be able to see them.'

– CAPTAIN BEEFHEART

'I understand there are Arabs who are not dirty.'
– PAUL RAND DIXON,
Federal Trade Commissioner

'Southern people just don't know Jews; all they know is
niggers. They regard Jews like Chinese; give 'em enough
rope and they'll start a rope factory.'   – KINKY FRIEDMAN

'But Nyasaland had only 8,000 whites against 3,000,000
blacks, and in these days (whatever your private feelings)
you cannot just go around shooting blacks by the score.'
– *Daily Mail*

'Frankly I don't like life without a subject race.'
– LADY REYNOLDS
who spent many years in India
in the *News Chronicle*

'They are just like us – hard to get to know but, underneath,
absolute dears.'   – SIR LAURENCE OLIVIER,
on the Poles

'Truly we have come to a pitiable pass when we have
Egyptians, Russians, Mexicans and a variety of Asiatics
claiming the ability to shape men's lives more wisely than
we can.'   – *Sunday Express*

'I can't even count on one hand five people of any importance in the media who aren't Jewish. I can't.'
– TRUMAN CAPOTE

'There are occasions when it is wise to disregard the old

counsel *de mortuis nihil nisi bonum*, and this is one of them. It is both appropriate and necessary to record that Freud's unhealthy obsession with sex has been responsible to an overwhelming extent for the depravity of mind and perversity of taste that has affected among others, English people and particularly English women since the last war. In itself a sufficiently grave evil, this result has had consequences immeasurably malignant, for it undoubtedly paved the way for wide acceptance of that complete Jewish ideology out of which sprang bolshevism, nazism and the present war.'
— Letter in *Lancet*

'What a po-faced lot these Dutch are!'
— DUKE OF EDINBURGH

'They asked me what I though of black power. I said black power is me making it with Aretha Franklin.'
— JUNIOR WELLS,
Bluesman

'I believe in white supremacy until the blacks are educated to a point of responsibility.'
— JOHN WAYNE

'The Americans ought to be ashamed of themselves for letting their medals be won by Negroes.'
— ADOLF HITLER

'I want to be the white man's brother, not his brother-in-law.'
— MARTIN LUTHER KING JR

'The haughty American nation . . . makes the Negro clean its boots and then proves the moral and physical inferiority of the Negro by the fact that he is a bootblack.'
— GEORGE BERNARD SHAW

'I am free of all prejudices – I hate everybody equally.'
                                                    – W. C. FIELDS

RELIGION

'Faith is under the left nipple.'   – MARTIN LUTHER

'For a priest to turn to a man when he lies a-dying, is just like one that has a long time solicited a woman, and cannot obtain his end, at length he makes her drunk, and so lies with her.'   – JOHN SELDEN

'All religions will pass, but this will remain – simply sitting in a chair and looking in the distance.'   – V. V. ROZANOV

'Christianity has done a great deal for love by making a sin of it.'   – ANATOLE FRANCE

'North Camden Deanery Synod's majority view is that there is no fundamental objection to the ordination of women priests. But not all its members agree. At a debate on the subject on Saturday, one curate declared: 'If God had meant women to be ordained, I would not have been born a little boy.'' '   – *Hampstead and Highgate Express*

'Clergyman: a ticket-speculator outside the gates of heaven.'   – H. L. MENCKEN

'Sunday: A day given over by Americans to wishing they

were dead and in heaven, and that their neighbors were
dead and in hell.'   – H. L. MENCKEN

'Theology: An effort to explain the unknowable by putting
it into terms of the not worth knowing.'   – H. L. MENCKEN

'The atheist confesses: Let us thank God there is no God.'
                                      – H. L. MENCKEN

'My feelings towards Christ are that he was a bloody good
bloke, even though he wasn't as funny as Margaret
Thatcher.'   – TERRY JONES
                                director of *The Life of Brian*

'I am one of those cliff-hanging Catholics. I don't believe
in God, but I do believe that Mary was his mother.'
                                    – MARTIN SHEEN, actor

'Different strokes for different folks. I sort of consider
myself a contemporary gadfly. The Universal Life Church
gives me a chance to dip my tail into the ointment and stir
up some shit.'   REV. KIRBY K. HENSLEY,
                          President of the Universal Life Church

'Crucifixes are sexy because they've got a naked man on
the front.'   – MADONNA

'We need a new cosmology. New Gods. New Sacraments.
Another drink.'   – PATTI SMITH

'Of course you are quite irreligious?'

'Oh, by no means. The fashion just now is a Roman Catholic frame of mind with an agnostic conscience: you get the medieval picturesqueness of the one with the modern conveniences of the other.'   – SAKI (H. H. MUNRO)

'What I got in Sunday School . . . was simply a conviction that the Christian faith was full of palpable absurdities, and the Christian God preposterous . . . The act of worship, as carried on by Christians, seems to me to be debasing rather than ennobling. It involves grovelling before a Being who, if He really exists, deserves to be denounced instead of respected.'   – H. L. MENCKEN

'Christianity might be a good thing if anyone ever tried it.'
     – GEORGE BERNARD SHAW

'All diseases of Christians are to be ascribed to demons.'
     – SAINT AUGUSTINE

'Mothers and dads that take their children to church never get into trouble.'   – J. EDGAR HOOVER

'I call Christianity the one great curse, the one enormous and innermost perversion, the one great instinct of revenge, for which no means are too venomous, too underhand, too underground and too petty – I call it the one immortal blemish of mankind.'   – FRIEDRICH NIETZCHE

'Faith must trample under foot all reason, sense, and understanding.'   – MARTIN LUTHER

'. . . no clergyman can nowadays attain high office who has not first given solid and continuous proof that he is ga-ga.'
– CLIVE JAMES

ROYALTY

'Nowadays a parlourmaid as ignorant as Queen Victoria was when she came to the throne would be classed as mentally defective.' – GEORGE BERNARD SHAW

'Perhaps the thing I might do best is to be a long distance lorry driver.' – PRINCESS ANNE

'This isn't ours. It's just a tied cottage.' – PRINCE PHILIP, on Buckingham Palace

'You know, the Queen really rather likes me.'
– KOO STARK

SCIENCE AND TECHNOLOGY

'Radio has no future.' – LORD KELVIN

'Electric light will never take the place of gas.'
– WERNER VON SIEMENS

'It can be exploited for a certain time as a scientific curiosity, but apart from that it has no commercial value.'

> – AUGUSTE LUMIÈRE,
> on the cinematograph (his own invention)

'If only I had known, I should have become a watch-
maker.'   – ALBERT EINSTEIN

'Man will never fly. Not in a thousand years.'

> – WILBUR WRIGHT (1900)

'If I had my life to live over again, I'd be a plumber.'

> – ALBERT EINSTEIN

'A thought that sometimes makes me hazy, Am I, or are
the others crazy?'   – ALBERT EINSTEIN

SELF

'You know, there's something about me that makes a lot of
people want to throw up.'   – PAT BOONE

'I'm the type of guy who'd sell you a rat's asshole for a
wedding ring.'   – TOM WAITS

'Neil Armstrong was the first man to walk on the moon. I
am the first man to piss his pants on the moon.'

> – BUZZ ALDRIN

'Let me die eating ortolans to the sound of soft music.'
— BENJAMIN DISRAELI

'To me, I'm just an ordinary English bloke, same as everyone else.' — MICK JAGGER

'I've never been a fan of personality-conflict burgers and identity-crisis omelets with patchouli oil. I function very well on a diet that consists of Chicken Catastrophe and Eggs Overwhelming and a tall, cool Janitor-in-a-Drum. I like to walk out of a restaurant with enough gas to open a Mobil station.' — TOM WAITS

'When I'm good I'm very good, but when I'm bad I'm better.' — MAE WEST

'I've been in *Who's Who* and I know what's what, but this is the first time I've been in a dictionary.' — MAE WEST
on becoming a life jacket

'Deep down underneath it all, I have the heart of a small boy. I keep it in a jar, on my desk.' — ROBERT BLOCH

'I've got a *monumental* conceit, *look* at me – conceit on the rampage. I seriously believe this: you've got to keep your conceit well-brushed and ready to operate at all times.'
— CLIVE JAMES

'I'm a tidy man. I keep my socks in the socks drawer and my stash in my stash box.' — GEORGE HARRISON (1969)

'If there is such a thing as genius, which is just what – what the fuck is it? – I am one, you know. And if there isn't, I don't care.'   – JOHN LENNON

'I too had thoughts once of being an intellectual but I found it too difficult.'   – ALBERT SCHWEIZER

'I'm a sort of Leonardo da Vinci of the rock business. I'm sure Leonardo would have understood me.'
                                                   – CHRIS SPEDDING

'When I get so annoyed over something, I need an enemy, somebody who's done something to me – so that I can take it out on them and beat them to a pulp. And I always find I'm sitting in a room with a load of friends and I can't do anything to them, so I just go upstairs and smash a glass and cut myself. The I feel better.'   – SID VICIOUS

'If I feel like killing a hippie, I will. I don't have to be angry to do that . . . I'm more of a robot than a person.'
                                                     – SID VICIOUS

'I get bored, you see. When I get bored, I rebel. I took out me 'atchet and chopped the 'otel room to bits. The lot of it. It happens all the time.'   – KEITH MOON, on his
                               infamous habit of destroying hotel rooms

'I've always been the one to push and shove and say, "Sorry, that's it darlin', it's all over, goodbye. Take twenty Valiums and have a stomach pump and that's the end of it."'   – ROD STEWART

'Fucking groupies. I'm telling you, the next one who pushes herself at me, I'm going to piss all over her . . . Wait till me mother reads that; she'll never speak to me again.'

– OZZY OSBOURNE,
Black Sabbath

'I'm like a woman because I have my periods, if you know what I mean. Every once in a while I get the cramps and do something far out.' – CAPTAIN BEEFHEART

'I wish I was with my friends tonight, destroying my hometown . . . You know, I stole seventeen cars in high school. I derailed a train with a rock. Me and my friends blew up all the thermostats in school with plastic explosives. We stole bowling balls and threw them into buildings from our cars at ninety miles an hour. We got rancid whipped cream from garbage cans at the Reddi-Whip factory and put it in fire extinguishers and sprayed it on people. It was the best time of my life.' – MARK MENDOZA,
The Dictators

'I'd like to autograph someone's face.' – SID VICIOUS

'If you're sitting around after a show and there's something you don't like, you just switch it off by throwing a bottle through the screen.' – KEITH MOON

'The only thing I regret about my life is the length of it. If I had to live my life again I'd make all the same mistakes – only sooner.' – TALLULAH BANKHEAD

'I'm the Connie Francis of rock and roll.' – ELTON JOHN

SEX

'I know nothing about sex, because I was always married.'
– ZSA ZSA GABOR

'A deadly dull day. To have to make love without feeling a particle is sad work, and sad and serious did I find it.'
– HENRY EDWARD FOX

'There is only one other profession that outranks bankers as dedicated clients, and that is the stockbroker . . . When the stocks go up, the cocks go up!'   – XAVIERA HOLLANDER

'You know the worst thing about oral sex? The view.'
– MAUREEN LIPMAN

'Make love to every woman you meet; if you get five per cent on your outlays it's a good investment.'
– ARNOLD BENNETT

'Conventional sexual intercourse is like squirting jam into a doughnut.'   – GERMAINE GREER

'I married a German. Every night I dress up as Poland and he invades me.'
– BETTE MIDLER

'I don't want to see any faces at this party I haven't sat on.'
– BONNIE RAITT

'I too have slept with Jack Kennedy.' – BETTE MIDLER

'The possibilities of heterosexuality are very nearly exhausted.' – Anonymous pornographer (1978)

'Virtue is its own punishment.' – ANEURIN BEVAN

'Anyone who was seduced wanted to be seduced.'
– MARLENE DEITRICH

'Sex is the invention of a clever venereal disease.'
– Sign in David Cronenberg's *Shivers*

'I feel like a million tonight – but one at a time.' – MAE WEST

'I'm saving the bass player for Omaha.' – JANIS JOPLIN

'People were always having love affairs with their poodles and putting tiny flowers in strange places.'
– ALICE ROOSEVELT LONGWORTH,
at age 90, reflecting on the sexual
morals of her own day

'A whore practicing fellatio looks up and says, "Are you a Communist?" – that's what the modern world is all about, in a way.' – NORMAN MAILER

'Most of my male friends are gay, and that seems perfectly natural to me. I mean, who wouldn't like cock?'
– VALERIE PERRINE

'Sex is a form of temporary insanity.'   – MARTIN GRIEF

'It is a common proverb in Italy that he knows not the perfect pleasure of Venus that hath not lain with a limping woman.'   – MONTAIGNE, *Essays*

'I could be content that we might procreate like trees, without conjunction, or that there were any way to perpetuate the world without this trivial and vulgar way of coition; it is the foolishest act a wise man commits in all his life.'   – SIR THOMAS BROWNE
Religio Medici

'All I ask of Thee, Lord/Is to be a drinker and a fornicator/ An unbeliever and a sodomite/And then to die.'
– CLAUDE DE CHAUVIGNY
17th-century poet,
'Blasphemer's prayer'

'Do you know why God hates homosexuality? Because the male homosexual eats another man's sperm. Sperm is the most concentrated form of blood. The homosexual is eating life.'   – ANITA BRYANT

'We believe that people should fuck all the time, anytime, whomever they wish. This is not a program demand but a simple recognition of the reality around us.'
– From a yippie pamphlet

'If homosexuality were the normal way, God would have made Adam and Bruce.'   – ANITA BRYANT

'I wake up every morning with a different girl in my bed. I think I must be suffering from jet slag.'   – GARY MOORE

'It's just handy to fuck your best friend.'   – JOHN LENNON,
on Yoko Ono

'I said to my boyfriend Ernie "Ya gotta kiss me where it smells." So he drove me to Wapping.'   – BETTE MIDLER

' "One can well understand those people who believe that intercourse is wrong except where children are concerned," the judge said. "That is a widely held and respectable view."
    'He added that the husband believed that intimacy was repellent, unpleasant and something to be endured in order to have children.'   – *News of the World*

'I was balling in cars up until the age of thirty before I knew what a bed was. It was wonderful. You never knew what was going to happen. It could be on a kitchen floor, whatever. It was this type of spontaneity you once could enjoy.'
    – TELLY SAVALAS

'A girl who says, "Pass me the fuckin' salt," "Pass me the fuckin' salad," "Pass me the fuckin' wine," and then says, "Let's go fuck" – by that time, who wants to?'
    – BURT REYNOLDS

'It is very hard to photograph the penis without it looking kind of depressing in three dimensions.'   – GORE VIDAL

'There will be sex after death – we just won't be able to feel it.'   – LILY TOMLIN

'Sexual behavior is just as common in Britain as in the US, according to a recent survey by Mass-Observation, a British research organization.'   – *The Scientific American*

'To my astonishment I find I am going to have a baby. I am just 18, and my boyfriend and I have never done anything but kiss and hold hands. Can you tell me how it happened?'
                                                              – *Woman's Own*

'Temptation is a woman's weapon and a man's excuse.'
                                                              – H. L. MENCKEN

'It takes all sorts to make a sex.'   – SAKI (H. H. MUNRO)

'Sex is the laughter of genius, it's the bathroom of your mind.'   – MALCOLM McLAREN

'I can't understand why more people aren't bisexual. It would double your chances for a date on a Saturday night.'
                                                              – WOODY ALLEN,
                                                              admitted heterosexual

'I tell the women that the face is my experience and the hands are my soul – anything to get those panties down.'
                                                              – CHARLES BUKOWSKI,
                                                              poet

'Any usage whatsoever of matrimony exercised in such a

way that the act is deliberately frustrated in its natural power to generate life is an offense against the law of God and of nature, and those who indulge in such are branded with the guilt of a grave sin.'   – POPE PIUS XI

'My method is basically the same as Masters and Johnson, only they charge thousands of dollars and it's called therapy. I charge fifty dollars and it's called prostitution.'
                                    – XAVIERA HOLLANDER

'I never thought of myself as a wicked brothel-keeper – I thought of myself as a welfare worker.'
                                    – MRS CYNTHIA PAYNE

'The erection of a penis is in itself a piece of natural mechanism of great interest and of human significance.'
                                    – GEORGE MELLY

'I take my vagina wherever I go. It belongs to me and I belong to it.'   – IRMA KURTZ

SOCIETY

'Most celebrated men live in a condition of prostitution.'
                                    – SAINT-BEAUVE

'There are persons who, when they cease to shock us, cease to interest us.'   – F. H. BRADLEY

'To be modern is to potter about in the terminal ward.'

– E. M. CIORAN

'The world is, for the most part, a collective madhouse, and practically everyone, however "normal" his façade, is faking sanity.'

– JOHN ASTIN

'There are only forty people in the world and five of them are hamburgers.'

– CAPTAIN BEEFHEART

SPORTS

'Games are the last resort of those who do not know how to idle.'

– ROBERT LYND

'World records are like shirts. Anyone can have one if he works for it.'

– FILBERT BAYI, Kenyan runner

'Winners aren't popular. Losers often are.'

– VIRGINIA WADE

'Show me a good loser in professional sports and I'll show you an idiot.'

– LEO DUROCHER, baseball manager

'Defeat is worse than death, because you have to live with defeat.'

– BILL MUSSELMAN, basketball coach

'Looking at a fighter who can't punch is like kissing your mother-in-law.'

– JACK HURLEY

'Yes, I agree, if I hadn't had so many defeats, I'd have been world champion.' – WINSTON BURNETT (boxed 88, lost 69)

'Football is a game designed to keep coal miners off the streets.' – JIMMY BRESLIN

'Rugby is a beastly game played by gentlemen; soccer is a gentleman's game played by beasts; football is a beastly game played by beasts.' – HENRY BLAHA

'Nobody is hurt. Hurt is in the mind. If you can walk, you can run.' – VINCE LOMBARDI, U.S. pro football coach

'A guy has a broken wrist: you hammer in there a few times, and you don't have no trouble with him for the rest of the night. It's nothing personal . . .' – PUNCH IMLACH, hockey player

'I do believe that my best hits border on felonious assault.' – JACK TATUM, U.S. pro football player

'I am convinced that if a fox could vote, he would vote Tory.' – Letter in *The Sussex Express and County Herald*

'If foxes could hear all sides of the debate on hunting, I think they would vote solidly for its continuance.' – *The Field*

'No man is fit to be called a sportsman wot doesn't kick his wife out of bed on a haverage once in three weeks.' – ROBERT SURTEES, *Jorrocks' Jaunts and Jollities*

'Watching an Americas Cup race is like watching grass grow.'
    – RING LARDNER

'England versus Scotland is not just a matter of life and death – it's more important than that.'
    – DAVID COLEMAN, sports commentator

'I promised I'd take Rotherham out of the second division. I did – into the third division.'
    – TOMMY DOCHERTY, ex-manager of Rotherham

'We murdered them. 0-0.'   – BILL SHANKLY, football manager

'It is vital, in my opinion, that tennis maintains a strong and watchful stand against swearing.'   – JOHN McENROE

'Sport is an armoured apparatus for coercion, an instrument of bourgeois hegemony in a Gramscian sense, dominated by a phallocratic and fascitoid idea of virility.'
    – JEAN-MARIE BROHM, French coach

'Louise Brough cannot serve at the moment because she has not got any balls.'   – REX ALSTON, tennis commentator

STYLE

'Like Joyce, I say: "Don't bother me with politics; the only thing that interests me is style".'   – JACK KEROUAC

'I used to think that if I could have a whole hot dog to myself, that would be style.'   – GLADYS KNIGHT

'It is not pansy to be elegant, just as it is not elegant to be pansy.'   – HARDY AMIES

'What is elegance: Soap and water!'   – CECIL BEATON

'Bad taste is, specifically, gladioli, cut-glass flower-bowls, two-tone motor cars and dollies to hide telephones. Good taste is, frankly, what *I* think is good taste.'   – DAVID HICKS

'I don't believe in style: I want to be a machine.'
– ANDY WARHOL

SUCCESS AND FAILURE

'Whenever a friend succeeds a little, something in me dies.'
– GORE VIDAL

'Celebrities are always rude to me – I can hardly think of one that has not, at one time or another, said rude things to me.'   – FORD MADOX FORD

'When you meet a public man who ostentatiously shortens his forename, make the sign of the Evil Eye and count your spoons.'   – BERNARD LEVIN

'In the future, everyone will be famous for fifteen minutes.'

– ANDY WARHOL

'You have to be a bastard to make it, and that's a fact. And the Beatles are the biggest bastards on earth.'

– JOHN LENNON

'Anybody seen in a bus after the age of thirty has been a failure in life.'   – LOELIA, DUCHESS OF WESTMINSTER

'Success always necessitates a degree of ruthlessness. Given the choice of friendship or success, I'd probably choose success.'   – STING, The Police

'The ultimate thing in a man's life is to get a damn good butler.'   – J. P. DONLEAVY

'Ah outlasted everyone else 'cause ah take vitamin 'E', baby.'   – ELVIS PRESLEY

'I'm in a class by myself, along with people like Rod Stewart.'   – ENGLEBERT HUMPERDINCK

'What am I supposed to do with the money I earn? Give it back?'   – ROD STEWART,
responding to criticism of his wealth
by the British punk bands

'It means that you have, as performers will call it, "fuck you" money . . . All that means is that I don't have to do what I don't want to do.'   – JOHNNY CARSON

'When you're as great as I am, it's hard to be humble.'
– MUHAMMAD ALI

'The higher a monkey climbs, the more you see of his ass.'
– GENERAL JOSEPH STILLWELL

'Every man has a right to be conceited until he is successful.'
– BENJAMIN DISRAELI

'Lots of people who complained about us receiving the MBE received theirs for heroism in the war – for killing people. We received ours for entertaining other people. I'd say we deserved ours more. Wouldn't you?'
– JOHN LENNON

'If at first you don't succeed, try, try, again. Then quit. There's no use being a damn fool about it.'   – W. C. FIELDS

TALK AND CONVERSATION

'I hate to spread rumours, but what else can one do with them?'
– AMANDA LEAR

'Remarks are not literature.'   – GERTRUDE STEIN

'Communication without purpose is artistic masturbation.'
– ROD STEIGER

'The voice is a second face.'   – GÉRARD BAUER

TELEVISION

'I like to talk on TV about those things that aren't worth writing about.'
— TRUMAN CAPOTE

'The ultimate game show will be the one where somebody gets killed at the end.'
— CHUCK BARRIS,
game show producer

'When you look at ideas for hundreds of programs, and they all happen to feature women with big bosoms, you know there's a trend.'
— LYNN ROTH,
director of TV Comedy Development,
20th Century Fox

'I had to go to bed at eight recently because I couldn't get a picture of any kind on my set.' — Letter to *Yorkshire Evening Post*

'We are having a couple to dinner next week who are very well connected and I am a little nervous. Is it correct to watch the telly both before and after dinner?' — Letter in
Evening Standard

'How can I get my two-year-old daughter interested in television? We sit her in front of the set. She watches for a few minutes and says: "Switch it off, Mummy." I should hate to think my daughter will grow up uninterested in TV.' — Letter in *Daily Mirror*

'You can feed your baby peacefully when it's cartoon time.'
— MARLENE DEITRICH

'Like, I can't be on none of those television shows, 'cause I'd have to tell Johnny Carson, "You're a sad mother-fucker." That's the only way I could put it.' – MILES DAVIS

'Television? No good will come of this device. The word is half Greek and half Latin.' – C. P. SCOTT,
Editor of the *Guardian*

'Television is for appearing on, not looking at.'
– NOEL COWARD

THEATER

'The first rule of the theater – give the best lines to yourself.'
– ROBERT BLOCH

'There are two kinds of directors in the theater. Those who think they are God and those who know they are.'
– RHETTA HUGHES

'The American theater is the aspirin of the middle classes.'
– WOLCOTT GIBBS

'Show me a congenital eavesdropper with the instincts of a Peeping Tom and I will show you the makings of a dramatist.' – KENNETH TYNAN

'All new plays are old plays.' – TOM STOPPARD

TRANSPORT

'The aeroplane will never fly.'   – LORD HALDANE (1907)

'The automobile changed our dress, manners, social customs, vacation habits, the shape of our cities, consumer purchasing patterns, common tastes and position in intercourse.'   – JOHN KETAS, *The Insolent Chariots*

'I see no reason to suppose that these machines will ever force themselves into general use.'
– THE DUKE OF WELLINGTON
on steam locomotives

'I tend to buy cars for the fun of it. I drive them around for three weeks and then I get bored, dump them in the garage and let the batteries go completely flat.'   – EDDIE MURPHY

'Space travel is utter bilge.'   – SIR RICHARD WOOLLEY,
Astronomer Royal (1956)

'I cannot conceive of any condition which would cause this ship to founder. I cannot conceive of any vital disaster happening to this vessel. Modern shipbuilding has gone beyond that.'   – E. J. SMITH, Captain of The *Titanic*

'Cursed is he that does not know the width of his car.'
– CHRISTOPHER DRIVER,
An Alternative Commination

TRAVEL

'It is not worthwhile to go around the world to count the cats in Zanzibar.'   – THOREAU

'Switzerland is my favorite place now, because it's so – nothing. There's absolutely nothing to do.'
     – ANDY WARHOL

'Italy is so tender – like cooked maceroni – yards and yards of soft tenderness ravelled round everything.'
     – D. H. LAWRENCE

'In Germany I found but little; and suffered, from six weeks of sleeplessness in German beds, &c &c, a great deal.'   – THOMAS CARLYLE

'If you want to know what it is to feel the "correct" social world fizzle to nothing, you should come to Australia.'
     – D. H. LAWRENCE

'Ireland is really a collection of secret socieites.'
     – V. A. PRITCHETT

'Israel – Hitler's revenge on the world.'   – ANON'

TUMBRIL TALK

'The supreme test of intelligence is the ability to live as one pleases without working.' – ERIC FRANK RUSSELL

'Most of us have stopped using silver every day.' – MARGARET THATCHER (1970)

'I am certain that the world needs contrast, and the slums supply it.' – RACHEL FERGUSON, in *Passionate Kensington*

'We want more autocrats. I am an autocrat, because by birth, breeding and intelligence I am fitted to lead,' – AUSTIN HOPKINSON, MP

'The post is hopeless and I have given up sending things by post. I have things delivered in my Rolls.' – BARBARA CARTLAND, quoted in *Sunday Express*

'I can't understand all the fuss about student grants. Carol managed to save out of hers. Of course, we paid for her ski-ing holidays.' – MARGARET THATCHER, quoted in the *Sun*

'There is only one form of the simple life – living at the Ritz Hotel and touching the bell.' – CECIL ROBERTS

WAR

'The quickest way of ending a war is to lose it.'
– GEORGE ORWELL

'I do not believe that civilization will be wiped out in a war fought with the atomic bomb. Perhaps two thirds of the people of the earth will be killed.' – ALBERT EINSTEIN

'Japan is not capable of war on a great scale. Japan represents a reservoir of a great revolutionary explosion.'
– LEON TROTSKY (1939)

'Artillery only seems effective against raw troops. Cavalry will have a larger sphere of action in future wars.'
– EARL HAIG

'The war situation has developed, not necessarily to Japan's advantage.' – Japanese Imperial Transcript
announcing surrender (1945)

'You always write it's bombing, bombing. It's not bombing. It's air support.' – COLONEL H. E. OPFER
USAF Attache, Phnom Penh

'It became necessary to destroy the town in order to save it.' – US Army Report on
the razing of Ben Tre (1968)

'From the Israeli point of view, it is the most humane siege of a city imaginable.'
— IZCHAK BEN-ARI,
Israeli Ambassador to West Germany,
on the bombing of Beirut (July 1982)

'We are confident that our presence in Lebanon has saved thousands of human lives.'
— YITZHAK SHAMIR,
Israeli Foreign Minister

WOMEN

'There are only two kinds of women – goddesses and doormats.'
— PABLO PICASSO

'Nature intended women to be our slaves. They are our property; we are not theirs. They belong to us, just as a tree that bears fruit belongs to a gardener. What a mad idea to demand equality for women! Women are nothing but machines for producing children.'
— NAPOLEON

'Despite my thirty years of research into the feminine soul, I have not been able to answer . . . the great question that has never been answered: what does a woman want?'
— SIGMUND FREUD

'I am an isolated Being on the Earth, without a Tie to attach me to life, except a few School-fellows and a score of females.'
— BYRON

'If she be faire, as the saying is, she is commonly a foole.'
— ROBERT BURTON

'Nature, I say, doth paynt them further to be weak, fraile, impacient, feble, and foolishe; and experience hath declared them to be unconstant, variable, cruell, and lacking the spirit of counsel and regiment.' – JOHN KNOX

'The five worst infirmities that afflict the female are indocility, discontent, slander, jealousy and silliness.'
– Confucian Marriage Manual

'God created Adam of all living creatures, but Eve spoiled it all.' – MARTIN LUTHER

'There's really no reason to have women on a tour unless they've got a job to do. The only other reason is to screw. Otherwise they get bored, they just sit around and moan.'
– MICK JAGGER

Q. 'What is woman of herself?'
A. 'A beast unperfect, given to ten thousand passions and pleasures, abominable to be thought well of; so that if men would do as they ought to do, they would not follow them nor pursue them, with other desires or appetite but as things inevitable, which necessity doth constrain them to use.' – *Delectable Demands* (1566)

'Women should be obscene and not heard.'
– JOHN LENNON

'I love being a woman. You can cry. You get to wear pants now. If you're on a boat and it's going to sink, you get to go on the rescue boat first. You get to wear cute clothes. It

must be a great thing, or so many men wouldn't be wanting to do it.'
                                                    – GILDA RADNER

'We all know that most women are built like pears.'
                                                    – JERRY SILVERMAN,
                                                    dress company president

'Lady Hylton-Foster, wife of Sir Harry Hylton-Foster, who became Speaker of the House of Commons last October, holds strong views on women members of Parliament. "I can't think why they do it," she tells me. "I just don't understand them. Women don't have enough education to become politicians."'   – *Sunday Express*

'When a woman becomes a scholar there is usually something wrong with her sex organs.'   – FREIDRICH NIETZSCHE

'Women should be struck regularly – like gongs.'
                                                    – NOËL COWARD

'When I glimpse the backs of women's knees I seem to hear the first movement of Beethoven's Pastoral Symphony.'
                                                    – CHARLES GREVILLE

'No woman marries for money, they are all clever enough, before marrying a millionaire, to fall in love with him first.'
                                                    – CESARE PAVESE

'Once a woman has given her heart you can never get rid of the rest of her.'   – VANBRUGH

'That girl in the omnibus had one of those faces of marvellous beauty which one sees casually in the streets but never among one's friends. Where do these women come from? Who marries them? Who knows them?' – THOMAS HARDY

'An intelligent woman is a woman with whom one can be as stupid as one wants.' – VALERY

'The way to a girl's mind is through her cunt.'
– RICHARD NEVILLE,
Play Power (1970)

'Mr Justice Boreham told her: "This is an exceptional case. You have shown yourself to be a good wife, a good mother and a good housewife and I cannot think of anything more one could say about any woman." ' – *Evening Standard*

'When women kiss it always reminds one of prize fighters shaking hands.' – H. L. MENCKEN

'Women do not like timid men. Cats do not like prudent mice.' – H. L. MENCKEN

'No matter how happily a woman may be married, it always pleases her to discover that here is a nice man who wishes she were not.' – H. L. MENCKEN

'Of course Celia shits! And how much worse if she didn't.'
– D. H. LAWRENCE

'Only Tammy Wynette and Alice Cooper know how hard it is to be a woman.'   – ALICE COOPER, on the
lyrics to his song 'Only Women Bleed'

'Of course we are not patronising women. We are just going to explain to them in words of one syllable what it is all about.'   – LADY OLGA MAITLAND,
Founder of 'Women for Peace',
in favour of nuclear deterrence

'Woman's greatest strength lies in being late or absent.'
– ALAIN

'I don't like strident women.'   – MARGARET THATCHER

WORK

'The only way anybody'd get me to work was to make the hours from one to two with an hour off for lunch.'
– MINNESOTA FATS, pool hustler,
who says he's never worked a day in his life

'You have to work with people, whatever assholes they might be.'   – RAQUEL WELCH

'How can I get to meet one of those grubby, ill-looking girls who wear cotton trousers and their hair all over their faces? I feel she would help to make my life less humdrum while I am learning to be a chartered accountant.'
– Letter in *Evening Standard*

'I pride myself on the fact that my work has no socially redeeming value.'
– JOHN WATERS

'Banking may well be a career from which no man really recovers.'
– J. K. GALBRAITH

'When two men in business always agree, one of them is unnecessary.'
– WILLIAM WRIGLEY JR

'A genius is one who can do anything except make a living.'
– JOEY ADAMS

'I am a sensitive writer, actor, director. Talking business disgusts me. If you want to talk business, call my disgusting personal manager.'
– SYLVESTER STALLONE,
on the card he hands out when approached
with business propositions

WRITERS AND WRITING

'The most important thing to remember about Shakespeare is that he was a writer, working on commission . . . I like to think that if the Bard were alive today he'd be out on the beach in Beverly Hills tapping out 'High Concept' Movies of the Week on his Wang Word Processor, up to his ruff in cocaine.'
– MAUREEN LIPMAN

'Virginia Woolf's writing is no more than glamorous knitting. I believe she must have a pattern book.'
– EDITH SITWELL

'I love being a writer. What I can't stand is the paperwork.'
– PETER DE VRIES

'A great many people now reading and writing would be better employed in keeping rabbits.' – EDITH SITWELL

'Every author really wants to have letters printed in the papers. Unable to make the grade, he drops down a rung of the ladder and writes novels.' – P. G. WODEHOUSE

'Literary fame is very limited; it's like being a famous taxidermist.' – IAN McEWAN

'The shelf life of the modern hardback writer is somewhere between the milk and the yoghurt.' – JOHN MORTIMER

'Having no talent is no longer enough.' – GORE VIDAL

'I sometimes feel sorry for writers, but normally I hate 'em.' – PAUL McCARTNEY

'They are the curse of the human race. Nine-tenths of the existing books are nonsense, and the clever books are the refutation of that nonsense. The greatest misfortune that ever befell man was the invention of printing.'
– BENJAMIN DISRAELI, *Lothair*

'Why has Wells spoiled one novel after another by dragging in these nasty subjects? Men of letters, in my experience, are not adulterers.' – DEAN INGE,
in the *Evening Standard*

'All a writer has to do to get a woman is to say he's a writer. It's an aphrodisiac.'   – SAUL BELLOW (1976)

'Ernest Hemingway: when his cock wouldn't stand up, he blew his head off. He sold himself a line of bullshit and bought it.'   – GERMAINE GREER

'Finishing a book is just like you took a child out in the yard and shot it.'   – TRUMAN CAPOTE

'A book is what they make a movie out of for television.'
    – LEONARD LOUIS LEVINSON,

'I think that Shakespeare is a shit. Absolute shit! He may have been a genius for his time, but I just can't relate to that stuff. "Thee and thous" – the guy sounds like a faggot.'
    – GENE SIMMONS, Kiss

'There is usually something wrong with the writers the young like.'   – ANTHONY BURGESS

'As one who has not read Karl Marx, who has no intention of reading Karl Marx and would far rather die than read Karl Marx, it is a little difficult for me to trace the precise nature of his influence on Shaw.'   – HESKETH PEARSON,
    Bernard Shaw

'I met Miss Enid Blyton, whose books for children have sold 40,000,000 copies, and asked her how she works. "Some writers plan chapters and work things out in advance," she said, "I just sit down and open the sluice gates and it just pours through."' — *Daily Express*

'With the single exception of Homer, there is no eminent writer, not even Sir Walter Scott, whom I can despise as entirely as I despise Shakespeare when I measure my mind against his. It would positively be a relief to dig him up and throw stones at him.'   – GEORGE BERNARD SHAW

'What is wrong with a little incest? It is both handy and cheap.'   – JAMES AGATE, reviewing *the Barretts of Wimpole Street*

'Jack Kerouac – that isn't writing, it's typing.'   – TRUMAN CAPOTE

'If I really knew how to write, I could write something that someone would read and it would kill them. The same way with music, or any effect you want – [it] could be produced if you were precise enough in your knowledge or technique.'   – WILLIAM BURROUGHS

'What a writer wants to do is not what he does.'   – JORGE LUIS BORGES

'Every man with a belly full of classics is an enemy of the human race.'   – HENRY MILLER

'Never lend books, for no one ever returns them; the only books I have in my library are the books that other folk have lent me.'   – ANATOLE FRANCE

'I never read a book before reviewing it. It prejudices one so!'
                                              – SYDNEY SMITH

YOUTH

'Youth lacks, to some extent, experience.' – SPIRO T. AGNEW

'You see, I've always been a bit more maturer than what I am.'
                                              – SAMANTHA FOX

'A youth with his first cigar makes himself sick. A youth with his first girl makes other people sick.'
                                              – MARY WILSON LITTLE

'We like to look sixteen and bored shitless.'
                                  – DAVID JOHANSEN of The New York Dolls

'The function of youth is to change laws made by old men for young men that old men would never break.'
                                              – IAN PAIGE

'Their sexual juices really start to flow at fourteen, fifteen and sixteen. It doesn't take much to provoke a guy. Whether you like it or not, a woman's a sex object, and they're the ones who turn the man on, generally.'
                           – JUDGE ARCHIE SIMONSON of Wisconsin,
                              refusing to sentence a 15-year-old boy for rape

'No shirt is too young to be stuffed.'   – LARRY ZOLF

'Our children will hate us too, y'know.'   – JOHN LENNON

ZANY

'Ninety per cent of *everything* is crap.'
– attributed to THEODORE STRUGEON

'We shall never understand each other until we reduce the language to seven words.'   – KAHLIL GIBRAN

'This makes me so sore it gets my dandruff up.'
– SAM GOLDWYN

HAIG: 'Because of the fluctuational predispositions of your position's productive capacity as juxtaposed to government standards, it would be momentarily injudicious to advocate an increment.'
AIDE: 'I don't get it.'
HAIG: 'That's right!'

'He heard a voice from heaven, saying "Drain-pipes!".'
– SAMUEL BUTLER

'He is a pelvic missionary. He's laid more ugly women than you'd ever believe. Ali wants to be liked. He has a great capacity to give and receive, and it carries over into exchanging bodies. He thinks the woman will remember it all her life.'   – DR FERNANDO PACHECO, Muhammed Ali's personal physician

'If I treat my body properly, I believe I'll live to 150.'
— MICHAEL JACKSON

'Believe me, today crocodiles are no longer crocodiles.'
— MAX ERNST

'I wake up laughing. Yes, I wake up in the morning and there I am just laughing my head off.'   — BRUCE WILLIS

'It is a fearful thing to contemplate that, when you are driving along the road, a heavy horse may at any moment drop from the sky on top of you.'
— MR JUSTICE VAISEY, reported
in *The Daily Graphic*

'But perhaps the universe is suspended on the tooth of some monster?'   — CHEKHOV

'Everything is worth precisely as much as a belch, the difference being that a belch is more satisfying.'
— INGMAR BERGMAN

INDEX